BAGHA JATIN

BAGHA JATIN

THE REVOLUTIONARY WHO TERRIFIED THE BRITISH

SOMENATH GUHA

An imprint of
Srishti Publishers & Distributors

Srishti Publishers & Distributors
A unit of AJR Publishing LLP
212A, Peacock Lane
Shahpur Jat, New Delhi – 110 049

editorial@srishtipublishers.com

First published by Bold,
an imprint of Srishti Publishers & Distributors in 2022

Copyright © Somenath Guha, 2022

10 9 8 7 6 5 4 3 2 1

This is a work of non-fiction, based on the author's thorough research of Indian history. Some events have been fictionalised for dramatic effect. While due care has been taken to verify all information at press time, any inadvertent miss brought to notice shall be updated in the subsequent editions.

The author asserts the moral right to be identified as the author of this work.

All rights reserved. No part of this publication may be reproduced, stored in a retrieval system, or transmitted, in any form or by any means, electronic, mechanical, photocopying, recording or otherwise, without the prior written permission of the Publishers.

Printed and bound in India

Dedicated to
Late Prashanta Kumar Bose,
a person I greatly admire and respect.

Grateful to
Late Arunava Lahiri,
for getting free access to his large collection
of books on freedom movement in India.

Contents

PRELUDE

It was in 1899 that Rudyard Kipling glorified Imperialism in his poem 'The White Man's burden'. He romanticized colonialism as the divine duty of the colonialists to serve and manage the half-civilized, under-developed people of the vanquished countries. But what happened in India is just the opposite! Within only a few decades, the White Man's rule became a huge burden for the country. India – from being a nation of abundant resources – turned to be a backyard of endemic poverty, hunger, famine and epidemics.

The East India Company sharks and the British government plunderers sucked the life-blood out of the ancient land's economy and reduced it to virtual penury. Such an extent of loot and exploitation has no parallel in history as well. It can be termed as an 'economic holocaust' coming on the heels of the rampant genocides that the vengeful colonisers had carried out as the reprisal for the War of Independence in 1857.

After the revolt had been comprehensively crushed, the next target of the British imperialists was to cripple the Indian economy. They were utterly brutal about their attitude towards India.

In 1875, Lord Salisbury, Secretary of State for India[1], put it most bluntly: *India must be bled.*[2] By the sixth and seventh decade of the nineteenth century, the country had begun to thrive in the cotton industry. In 1856, a person named Cowaszee Nanabhoy Davar (1815-1873) started a cotton mill in Bombay (now Mumbai). It was known as the 'Bombay Spinning and Weaving Company' and laid the foundation of the industry in India. In 1866, there were 13 mills, which rose to 51 in 1877. By the end of the century, the number of mills operating in the country became 156. Most of these mills were in Bombay; others were in Ahmedabad, Sholapur, Kanpur, Madras (now Chennai) and Calcutta (now Kolkata).

Out of the many industries that had come up during this period, only the cotton mills were almost exclusively owned by the Indians. Indian fabric flourished in Europe and became a real competitor for British manufacturers. As a consequence, the British merchants, particularly the Lancashire mill owners, became concerned. They began to pressurize their government in India to impede the growth of the local cotton industry.

Already, in 1852, import duties on British cotton, silk and woolen garments were reduced drastically. On the other hand, all arrangements were made for unhindered export of raw materials from India to England. This policy

---

1 British Cabinet Minister and the political head of the India Office.

2 Sakharam Ganesh Deuskar, 2016.

proved to be the proverbial death nail for the Indian industries, particularly cotton. It was handicapped by the lack of raw materials. It resulted in the products becoming much costlier, making it almost impossible to compete with the cheap British fabric which flooded the Indian market. The ruthlessness with which the British strangled Indian industries can be understood from the government policies pursued during this time.

In 1879, import duty on British cotton was eliminated by Viceroy Lytton.[3] It deprived the government of the much-needed revenue, that too at a time when four consecutive famines had occurred between 1867 and 1877. The heartlessness of the government policy can be measured by the fact that more than six million people[4] are said to have died in the 1877 famine alone. By 1882, British goods were exempted from all import duties, making India a monopoly market for the English merchants. Over and above this, 5% excise tax was imposed on all cloth manufactured in India.[5]

Needless to say, British policies not only strangled Indian industries, but also caused unprecedented misery for the Indian people. Ever since the Battle of Plassey, rampant and all-pervasive famines had been a recurring feature in the country. The great Bengal famine in 1770 – in which nearly one crore people are said to have perished[6] – is all too well known. What is lesser known is the general scarcity

---

3 https://api.parliament.uk/historic-hansard/lords/1905/mar/13/import-duties-in-india. Accessed in September 2022.

4 David Fieldhouse, 1996. Pp. 400, pp. 108–146.

5 Suprakash Roy, 1949. Pp. 3-10.

6 Vinita Damodaran, 2014. Pp. 80–101, 89.

and unavailability of food, and the resultant hunger, that existed through the 19th century.

In the first twenty-five years of the 19th century, close to ten lakh people died due to hunger. Between 1826 to 1850, deaths due to hunger came down to five lakhs. In the third quarter of the century, when British rule was cemented after their victory in the 1857 War of Independence, there were six famines in India, in which fifty lakh people perished. And in the last quarter, when imperialists' rule was strengthened and took roots throughout the country, when exploitation had reached unbridled proportions, there were 18 famines in which a staggering two crores and sixty lakh people perished. Out of this, one crore and ninety lakh people died in the last decade alone.[7]

Thus, British policies not only hindered local industries, but also resulted in catastrophic hunger, poverty. This led to crores of deaths in only about a century of imperialists' rule. After the Government of India Act of 1858, administration of the country shifted from the directors of the company to a Secretary of State advised by a council. They, in turn, ruled the country with the help of one thousand five hundred civil servants. These were exclusively British, as no Indian was allowed into the Indian Civil Service (ICS).

This was another point of contention for the Indians. The hostile attitude of the British towards Indian industries, restrictions on Indians to enter various services, highhandedness of the British towards the local educated people led to much resentment among the affluent class,

7 Suprakash Roy, 1949. Pp. 26-27.

mostly comprising big landlords and businessmen. This found expression in the formation of the 'British Indian Association' in 1851. One of its founders was Maharshi Debendranath Tagore, father of Rabindranath Tagore, and among the members were eminent writer and journalist Pyarichand Mitra and Harish Chandra Mukhopadhya.[8] At the same time, 'Bombay Association' was established, led by the likes of Dadabhai Naoroji. Similar organizations also came up in Puna (now Pune) and Madras. It is important to note that some of the main demands of all these organizations included support for Indian manufacturers, reducing British monopoly on trade, inclusion of Indians in the civil service, protection of life and property of the masses and education for the people.

Due to vociferous demand, Indians were allowed to compete in the ICS exam eventually. But this was mostly a token concession; the minimum age at which one could sit for the exam was 17 and maximum, 22. Moreover, one had to go to England to sit for the exam. By 1869, only one Indian had been able to crack the exam. By 1878, the process was made even tougher by reducing the upper age to 19.

On the other hand, increasing trade and business required more clerks, employees and small time workers. Earlier on, the demand was met by the influx of young men from Britain and local Eurasians and Anglo-Indians. To meet this demand, more schools and colleges were opened to educate and prepare local people for these jobs. More

---

8 https://en.banglapedia.org/index.php/British_Indian_Association,_The. Accessed in July 2022.

educational institutes required more teachers; more mills and factories required more skilled workers and employees. As a result, an educated middle-class, however subservient, developed in the country.

Even with this rapid expansion of trade and education, jobs were few in comparison to the huge number of job-seekers. As a result, unemployment became rampant. For the few who were fortunate to land a job, wages were low and working conditions, miserable. All the top posts in any government or private enterprise were monopolized by the British. Their attitude towards the subordinate Indians was abominable.

People in the countryside were even more distressed. The introduction of railways transported foreign goods to the interiors, in a way destroying indigenous handicrafts. Artisans, weavers, potters or people engaged in rural non-agricultural occupations were rendered jobless. It has been estimated that by the end of the 19th century, almost three-fourths of the population came to depend on agriculture.

Just when people were reeling under severe exploitation, the indigo cultivators revolted. In large parts of the Bengal Presidency, peasants were forced to cultivate indigo instead of their traditional crops. The indigo-planters were ferocious in their approach. Their methods of persecution spread terror in the villages. They didn't tolerate any dissent and didn't hesitate to physically subjugate anyone who opposed their methods. But even the most inhuman oppression has its limits. The ryots (peasants) decided to strike back and stopped cultivating indigo.

In a significant turnaround, the Bengali intelligentsia – which had been somewhat muted during the 1857 revolt – now came out openly in favour of the ryots. Harish Chandra Mukhopadhya was most strident in his criticism of the planters in his newspaper, *Hindu Patriot*. Others like Nabagopal Ghosh and Sisir Ghosh were equally vocal. Dinabandhu Mitra wrote the path-breaking drama *Nil Darpan*. The trial concerning the publication of this drama caused a sensation in the society. In the face of mounting opposition from influential sections, and of course the cultivators, the government was forced to set up the Indigo Commission in 1860. According to the report of the Commission, indigo cultivation was gradually phased out, though it continued to flourish in some remote pockets even into the second decade of the twentieth century.

The success of this revolt led to a spurt in the publications of various types of periodicals in the coming decade. These did not merely pander to British whims and fancies. Some – like *Somprakash* – were most vocal in their criticism of British policies. Even regional newspaper like *Dhaka Darpan* became strident in opposing government policies. The patriotic fervour expressed by these newspapers became a concern for the administration. They instituted the Vernacular Press Act in 1878[9] and gagged the local press. But the English newspapers continued their tirade against foreign rule. Foremost among these were the *Amrita Bazar*

9 https://www.britannica.com/topic/Vernacular-Press-Act. Accessed in September 2022.

Patrika, Bengalee, Hindu Patriot, Hindu in Madras and *Kesri* in Bombay.

This patriotic fervour, together with the rising misery of the masses, led to the formation of the Indian Association in 1876. It was founded by Surendranath Banerjee and Ananda Mohan Bose, and was the first organization in the country which was spread across various provinces. It was basically a middle class organization led by educated young men, teachers, lawyers, writers, etc.

The Association was the first organization ever to hold an all India conference with representatives from every province. Surendranath can be credited as being the first leader with an all India stature. The organization's singular great characteristic was its religion-neutral outlook. One of its main objectives was the promotion of friendly relations between Hindus and Muslims. This is important to note, as it was a time when every organization was hugely influenced by religion. Later, the Association merged with the Indian National Congress. Strangely, it was the affluent, suave, English-educated, British-friendly leaders of the INC – generally known as Moderates – who were more unprejudiced religion-wise than the Extremists who were uncompromising in their opposition to the colonialists, but highly conservative and parochial in religious matters.

Religion held sway over patriotism. It was proved by the fact that a 'Hindu Mela' was organized in Calcutta on the day of the Chaitra Sankranti, in April 1867.[10] For the first three years, it was known as the Chaitra Mela. It was

10 Sailendra Nath Sen, 2010. P. 235.

initiated by Rajnarayan Basu, a respected social reformer of the time, and Nabagopal Mitra. Members of the Tagore family were involved with the organization at various stages. Rabindranath recited a poem at the mela sometime in the mid-seventies.

It was organized to revive the glorious past of the Hindus, to rekindle interest in the Bengali language and to resist western culture and values. Informally, though, it was intended to raise awareness against colonial rule by using religion as a tool. Rural handicrafts, indigenous art and craft, and locally manufactured products were displayed during the mela. *Lathi-khela* and various physical exercises were on show. Cultural soirees were held in the evenings. Patriotic songs were sung, poems recited and various forms of folk art and theater were presented. In that way, the Hindu Mela was a precursor to the Swadeshi movement. This formula of using religion to propel patriotism was used by Bal Gangadhar Tilak when he started Ganesh Utsab and Shibaji Utsab in Bombay in the 1890s.

While organizations like the Indian Association relied on legal and constitutional methods to oppose the colonialists, more extreme and violent methods were being devised to fight the British simultaneously. It was around this time that secret societies were being formed, which would go on to play a significant role in the liberation of the country. Surendranath Banerjee was said to have been involved in some of these societies.

One of the most significant of these societies is the Sanjibani Sabha, of which Rabindranath Tagore himself has reminisced. The poet was introduced to this group by his elder brother Jyotirindranath, when he was merely a teenager. The President of the society was Rajnarayan Basu, and here too, Nabagopal Mitra was a member. The poet has described the proceedings of the society which was held at a dilapidated house in north Calcutta. In a dimly-lit room, the President would read out the oath to every member. It is said that a human skull used to be kept on the table and blood would be drawn from the body to be used as offering. Needless to say, the atmosphere was eerie.

It was in this milieu of poverty, famine, joblessness and colonial exploitation, juxtaposed against an incipient rise of patriotism which crystallized into various forms of anti-British organizations, that our hero was born. His life encompassed nearly three-and-a-half decades, during which British faced relentless opposition to their rule, for the first time since 1857.

A DEVOUT AND DARING VILLAGE BOY

Almost a hundred and fifty miles from Calcutta, remote and forlorn in the Nadia district of the then united Bengal, there nestled a village named Koya. The nearest town was Kusthia. The entire region, which was then eastern Bengal, is now a part of Bangladesh. The area was abundantly agricultural, with vast fields of paddy and jute criss-crossing with overflowing rivers. During monsoon, the entire area turned into a sprawling swamp and the interior became almost inaccessible. Even the creeks and streams brimmed over, presenting a picturesque sight. A variety of water-crafts like *dinghy*, canoe, sailing boat and the occasional steamer danced merrily on the turbulent waves.

Koya is situated by the river Gorai – a humble tributary of the mighty Padma river, which rumbles three miles away. Its water inundated the shores of the village and ran into its muddy paths and alleys. It was a modest village with thatched huts and tin-roofed single-storied houses.

Poverty and disease was then the hallmark of most Bengal villages. People generally lived hand to mouth, not knowing where the next meal would come from. Famines were a recurring phenomenon and so were epidemics, with people suffering from a host of diseases like cholera, malaria, diarrhoea and unknown fevers. There was a feeling of gloom when one entered Koya, soon dispelled away by the banter of children playing in the mud and the merry laughter of women going about their chores.

Amidst the general impoverishment, the sprawling estate of the Chatterjees stood majestically, aloof and luminous. The property was spread around several acres. There was a large garden of coconut, mango, jackfruit and palm trees, along with a variety of vegetables. There was also a cowshed, stable and an *akhada*[11]. The mansion itself had numerous rooms, a *baithak khana*[12], kitchens, large courtyards and long, unending verandahs.

On 7th December 1879, Sharatshashi Mukherjee, the daughter of the Chatterjee family, gave birth to a boy in one of the secluded rooms of the mansion. He was named Jatindranath Mukherjee, who through his daring exploit in later years acquired the nickname *Bagha Jatin*.

It is not known if Umeshchandra Mukherjee, the father of the newborn, had reacted in the way we are accustomed to seeing in the movies. It is not known if he had rushed to the room hearing the baby's cries, and looking at the face of his son, if he had beamed in delight. What is known is that a few days before his untimely death, he had reminded Sharatshashi of the illustrious histories of both

---

11 An area for physical exercises, wrestling, lathi-khela, fencing, etc.

12 Drawing room.

the Mukherjee and Chatterjee families. He had said that a *pundit* had prophesied that born at an auspicious hour, his son would be of rare quality, would grow up to be a gifted human being and would not only add prestige to their families, but also bring glory to the country.

The Chatterjees were five brothers – Basanta Kumar, Hemanta Kumar, Anathbandhu, Durgaprasanna and Lalit Kumar. Sharatshashi, born a year after the first war of independence, in 1858, was younger to Basanta and Didi to the other brothers. She was married to Umeshchandra, who belonged to Rishkhali village of Jhinaidaha sub-division of Jessore district. Umeshchandra was a man of character, spirited and dignified.

Those were the days when indigo cultivation was thriving in Bengal, particularly in the districts of Jessore, Nadia and Khulna. There was an indigo factory at a village called Sidre quite near to Rishkhali. The planters, the white sahibs were omnipotent. No law could restrain them, and the police and the administration was at their beck and call. They were ferocious and merciless in their dealings with the locals, particularly the peasants.

The planter at Sidre always rode on a horse. Whoever happened to cross his path, had to bow his head in obeisance. Even *zamindars*[13], traders and local elders dismounted from their palanquins to show their respect. Umeshchandra was an exception, though. He walked past with his head held high and the planter dare not intimidate him.

---

13 A land owner, who lets it out to tenant farmers.

Umeshchandra and Sharatshashi had four children. Their eldest son died at the age of two years. Umeshchandra passed away in 1884 at the young age of thirty-four, leaving behind his daughter Binodbala (aged ten) and two sons – Jatin (five years) and Surendranath (one year). Umeshchandra was not a moneyed man and Sharat with her three children was in dire straits after his sudden demise. But her brothers, particularly Basanta and Hemanta Kumar, promptly came to her rescue. They took the family away to Koya and settled them in a part of the family mansion. They gave Sharat utmost respect and she virtually became the matriarch of the house.

Jatin grew up in the same house, with his cousins. As he grew older, he hardly retained any memory of his father. Though events in later years would prove that the boldness and defiance of Umeshchandra ran in his veins.

The young Jatin was not particularly naughty. In fact, he was rather timid. For instance, as a child, he was quite scared of dogs. It is quite common for children to feel that fear, but Sharat knew that given the tough circumstances, Jatin had to be stronger.

One day when his mother was cooking, Jatin came running and fell into her lap. Before Sharat could ask him what the matter was, he muttered something about a dog chasing him. His eyes were bulging with fear, almost on the verge of tears.

Sharat showed no sympathy and asked him to head out. She even gave him a piece of burning log.

"Go! Go and chase the dog! Don't return until you do it," she said strictly.

Jatin hesitated. But when he saw that his mother meant what she said, he ran after the dog. He ran a few steps and the hapless animal slunk away. Jatin came back smiling, conquering his fear forever.

Jatin's sister Binodbala recalls that this was perhaps the only instance when she saw her brother being frightened. In fact, Sharat was quite tough when it came to raising her son. From the smallest of chores around the house, to physical activities, she was careful about his overall development.

The way she taught the boy to swim became folklore in the village. Usually during the monsoon season, river Gorai became menacing; its waves swift and mighty. One didn't even dare approach the banks of the river at such times. But Sharat was made of different stuff. She would take the boy to the river, tie him up with one end of her saree and fling him into the water.

"Come on Jatin, swim harder! You can do it! You must reach the other side. Beat the current… yes, you're doing it right! You can do it!" she continuously egged him on.

Only when she saw Jatin struggling against the torrential waves, she would rush to him with swift strokes. But she wasn't done yet. Once in the water with him, she would continue the lesson.

"Look at me closely. See how I am doing it. Watch!"

She herself would wade into the water and negotiate the waves with rapid strokes. Jatin would look at her with awe and longed for the day when he would be as good as her.

This was an everyday routine in their lives. No wonder that within a few months, the child began to swim the entire length and breadth of the river. He would dive under a massive wave, and moments later, float on top of it. He would cross villages and float away miles afar.

The villagers, though, were not amused. They would rebuke Sharat for being so merciless, pushing the boy to the brink of death.

But she was unperturbed with all the criticism. She knew what she was doing, and would tell everyone, "You will see, he would grow up and swim across rivers as big as Padma and Meghna someday."

Jatin never looked back thereafter. His strength, courage and curiosity to know the world increased in leaps and bounds.

His *mamas*[14] nourished his character. The eldest uncle, Basanta Kumar, was a lawyer at Krishnanagar. He was a distinguished person known for his honesty and integrity. He was wealthy, but very charitable, always willing to help the poor and downtrodden.

The other uncle, Hemanta Kumar, lived at Sovabazar in Calcutta. He was a renowned doctor and just as generous and philanthropic as his elder brother. His house at Sovabazar was a veritable *dharmashala* where any student who came from Koya and nearby villages could get free food and shelter.

But the key figure behind the development of both Binodbala and Jatin was their mother Sharatshashi. She was

---

14 Maternal uncles.

clearly ahead of her times in many ways. She was pious and could be stern as well as affectionate. Initially, her husband's death had rattled her beyond measure. And why wouldn't it! Given the responsibilities she had. But when she was honorably settled in her paternal house, she put her mind and soul in raising her three children. After the untimely death of her youngest son Surendranath at the age of two, she was shaken. Eventually, she married off Binodbala at the age of eleven, with Surendranath Gangopadhyay of Chakda in Nadia district.

Misfortune continued to stalk her as her daughter was widowed even before attaining adulthood. Her husband died two years after they were married. She returned to her mother at her maternal uncles' house and never married again. Undaunted by the recurring tragedies, Sharat decided to give the children proper education. Later on in her life, Binodbala studied in the Victoria School in Calcutta. She became adept in both Bengali and English, and even became a teacher at Carmichael Girls' School in Krishnanagar.

Sharat was an avid reader herself. She read a wide variety of books. She read the *Gita*, the epics *Mahabharat* and *Ramayana*, and also the modern masters like Bankim Chandra Chattopadhya, Michael Madhusudan Dutta, Bhudeb Mukherjee and several others. Her reading habit instinctively led her to become a good poet. But rather than honing her own skills, she was keen to share her knowledge with others, particularly her children.

Whenever she found time, she read out from these books to them. At night, during bedtime, they would snuggle up to her and hear stories of Maharana Pratap, Shivaji or Pratapaditya. On some other evenings, she would read out tales of Sri Chaitanya, Kabir and other luminaries of the Bhakti cult. She was popular, the cynosure of the women of the village. Many of them attended her reading sessions. She helped them in their daily chores and would always walk the extra mile to help the needy. Often, she would give away her clothes and food to people in distress.

As is natural, all these qualities rubbed on her son. Jatin's curiosity was anyway boundless. So he read extensively and observed people around him to gather more about life.

Those were the days when letters were delivered by mail-runners. At Koya, a runner would occasionally come from Kusthia with letters and articles. His name was Bhuimali. Jatin fondly called him Bhuimalida. He was a tall, rickety man, jogging briskly with a bag over his shoulders. He had a lance in his hand to protect himself from wild animals. Bells were attached to the tip of the lance, the jingle of which heralded his arrival. As soon as Jatin heard the ringing sound, he would rush out of the house to meet the postman. Bhuimali would sit under a large tree, wipe away his sweat and ask for a sip of water. Villagers would gather around him, smoke their *hukkah* and prod the runner about affairs in nearby villages. Others would enquire if he had any letters for them.

When the crowd thinned, Jatin would get closer to Bhuimali and ask him about his experiences. Having rested and satisfied the villagers, Bhuimali would turn his attention to the boy. He would bare all his experience to the ever curious Jatin. The little boy had unending questions. How far was he coming from? Had he come across any wild animal on the way? Did he have a fight? Was there any crematorium on his way? Did he see burning corpses? Were there ghosts at these places? And with wide, inquisitive eyes, he would wonder aloud, did he not feel afraid travelling alone?

"Afraid, why! I have this lance na!" The postman would reply merrily. "And ghosts? There are no ghosts."

"But people here say that there are ghosts, all kinds of apparitions…at the burning ghat," Jatin would ask fearfully. "And there must be wild animals? Are you not afraid of them?"

The postman would burst into laughter and wrap him in an embrace. He would painstakingly dispel all his fears. "I will take you with me one day, *baba*. You will see for yourself that there are no ghosts, no animals."

Bolstered by the postman's sincere and loving assurances, one afternoon Jatin declared to his mother that he was going to the burning ghat to find out for himself whether there were really any ghosts or not. Sharat was a bit apprehensive, but she was not one to hold back her child. Jatin went to the crematorium and found one or two burning corpses. Dogs and jackals were sniffing around for a bite and occasionally breaking into blood-chilling howls. But there were no ghosts, no incorporeal beings that would jump from the trees and wring his neck apart. Jatin didn't feel afraid. After moving around for a while, he returned home and animatedly described his adventure to his mother and sister.

He was also curious of the railway bridge over the Gorai river. It was a swiftly flowing river with a strong current. Everyone was aware how every monsoon, the river became menacing and its water often swept away home and hearth. Then, how had humans built such a huge structure on this torrential river, Jatin would often ask incredulously.

The elderly people explained to him how the white men came and brought with them large number of coolies. They would describe to him the herculean struggle between man and nature. Portions of the bridge were built and then suddenly a huge tide of the river washed it away. This happened time and again. Exhausted by the inhuman struggle, many coolies tried to run away from the site. They were mercilessly shot down by security guards. Building of the bridge had cost many lives, the village elders often sighed.

Jatin fell silent on knowing this. Who knows, maybe a resolve grew in his mind at that tender age to avenge the deaths of the hapless coolies some day in the future!

Jatin's schooling was also going steadily along with the practical learning he got from Sharat. He was admitted to the primary school in the village soon after the family settled at Koya. He performed well in studies and grew in strength and stature. He picked up various skills from his uncles too. Since he was deeply observant as a child, he used to pick up qualities and ways to work his way around from everyone he saw closely.

His *mama,* Basant Kumar had a passion for horses and he presented an Arabian stead to the boy. These types of horses are very powerful and energetic. But in no time, Jatin began to handle it expertly. There was a road by the side of his house, which went as far as Kumarkhali. Jatin used to practice riding on this road. Often he would do away with the reins and saddle, and holding the horse by the tuft of hair on its neck spur it to run at a high speed on the empty stretch ahead.

The villagers looked at this wondrous boy and marvelled how even at the age of ten he had become so skilled and powerful. There are pictures of him holding a horse by its reins, bright and healthy and looking at the world with his large, expressive eyes.

As he grew up, he came into closer contact with his other maternal uncles – Anathbandhu and Lalit Kumar. The former was an agent of the Maharaja of Nadia and also an assistant translator attached with the Bengal government. He had a rifle and taught Jatin how to use it. Within a few months, he became an expert at it too. From his youngest uncle Lalit Kumar, he learned to row a boat.

With all these qualities, it was inevitable that he became the leader of the boys in the village. They formed a football club and played matches in the neighbouring villages. He formed a Seva Dal to help the sick and the elderly. Whenever they heard of someone being sick and living all alone, Jatin and his friends would reach out to help. They would arrange doctors and medicine, and stay over at nights to look after the patient.

Life was going smoothly for the family. One year later, the epidemic of cholera engulfed the area. In those days, cholera was highly infectious and had a high mortality rate. People rarely dared to go close to a patient. It was tough for infected people to do anything, leave alone caring for themselves. But the fear that engulfed his fellows didn't deter Jatin even one bit. Charged with the zeal of community service, he immediately went into action. He cajoled or coerced his classmates to help him in this endeavour.

So every time they got to know of a person who was suffering from cholera, the boys would go forth and help in whichever way they could. It is really worth noting how even at such a young age, he was always willing to help people in distress.

As discussed earlier, this was a time when English-medium schools were set up across the country. Since there were no English-medium schools at Koya, he was taken to Krishnanagar by Basanta Kumar at the age of twelve. His uncle was already reputed and well-established in the town, so Jatin did not have to face any difficulty with the admission.

He was admitted to the famous Anglo Vernacular school in the town. Since Jatin was a dedicated child, he put his heart and mind into learning. He had developed a keen interest in physical exercises in the past few years. But since there was no gymnasium in the school, he was unable to practice suitably. He found out that a college situated nearby had a well- equipped gymnasium. But it was only meant for college students and Jatin still had a few years to reach that level. But no problem ever seemed insurmountable to this boy.

One day, he went to visit the European principal of the college. He spoke in broken, pidgin English and sought his permission to use the gymnasium. This was very unusual in those days. Not to talk of a teenager, even adults were wary of going near a white man, leave alone speaking to him.

The principal looked up. A young boy, healthy and bright, stood in front of him. He was impressed. The very fact that a village boy had the courage to come and speak to him amazed him.

"Where are you from?" he asked.

"Koya village," pat came the instant reply.

"Which school?" the principal again raised his eyes, a faint smile at the edge of his mouth.

Jatin answered him politely. He was calm, without an iota of nervousness. There was momentary silence.

"You are most welcome," the elderly man finally broke into a smile. "And you are also welcome to come and meet me whenever you feel like."

This was quite encouraging for Jatin and only added to his confidence. On the other hand, when his uncle Basanta Kumar came to know what had happened, he knew that Jatin was keen on body-building sincerely. So he went forth and engaged an ex-army man from Peshawar, who was also an excellent wrestler. His name was Feraz Mian.

Jatin and his cousins were regularly trained by Feraz Mian, who hailed from India's western frontiers. He taught them various martial arts and also inculcated courage in them. Jatin was captivated by this man's personality. He was charming and freedom-loving, a trait which influenced Jatin greatly. These two developments heralded Jatin's mission of building up a robust and vigorous physique, which he was to pursue throughout his life. He began to treat his body as a shrine – a trait that would be picked up by young men of Bengal a few years later, leading to trailblazing consequences.

As Jatin was developing into an exciting young man quite oblivious of what destiny had in store for him, India was slowly rising out of the slumber it had immersed into since 1857. The publication of *Anandamath* in 1882 by Bankim Chandra Chattopadhyay, the great litterateur, electrified the young men of Bengal. The euphoria later spread to the rest of the country as well. The call of *Bande Mataram* caused a spark in people's consciousness, unprecedented in recent times.

The prelude of the novel itself is enigmatic and elevating. It's dramatic. A man is in quest, wandering through a forest spread over miles of unpopulated land. It is deep, dense and dark. Large trees like sal entwine with each other so thickly and inseparably that even sun rays cannot penetrate through. The woods are opaque, bereft of light, and even in daytime, immersed in perpetual darkness. The man meanders through it in the middle of the night. Millions of birds, insects and animals that inhabit the land are in a slumber. It is pitch dark and wrapped in absolute silence.

Into this void of darkness and soundlessness, the man raises his voice and pleads, "Will my desire not be fulfilled?" His words are lost in that sea of silence. He repeats and again there is no reply to his query. His words echo through the jungle, causing the silence to become even more eerie. When he asks for the third time, a voice answers, "What do you promise in return?"

"My life, the entirety of it," the man says.

"Life is a trifle! Everyone can renounce it," the unseen voice boomed.

"What more do I have, what more can I promise?" the man beseeches helplessly.

"Bhakti," the mysterious voice reverberates and gives his ultimate verdict.

It is this 'bhakti' which has since then caused much debate. What did the author mean by it? The predominant opinion is that it is devotion to the motherland. Motherland doesn't just mean a piece of land or the people residing there. Motherland is Mother herself, in the real sense; more importantly, in its spiritual sense. It is a feeling, an all engulfing emotion to which the self surrenders itself, soul and body, and prepares for its upliftment and emancipation.

Ananadamath can be considered as a rebuff to the British propaganda championed by the imperialist Thomas Babington Macaulay. It refutes the theory that the British are an esteemed, superior race and that India is an obscurantist society steeped in deep superstitions and archaic feudal practices. This supremacist attitude of the sahibs ashamed the rising Indian middle class. To counter this, Indian reformers and litterateurs, who were mostly upper caste Hindus, invoked the glory of India's ancient past. And that glory being synonymous with the Sanatan Dharma, equating the Motherland with Devi became inevitable. While this created a wave of patriotism, it also alienated sections of Muslim population who understandably were not comfortable with the country being looked upon as a Devi.

Jatin had read *Anandamath* when he was in high school. He was so touched with the various aspects of the narrative that he read it time and again. So much so, that he had almost memorized it. He believed one could not realize the essence of patriotism if not initiated into the creed described in the novel.

The young men of Bengal would mould themselves as '*santans*', the children of the Mother and prepare themselves with unprecedented zeal for her liberation. The novel laid the foundation of Indian nationalism, an amalgamation of patriotism and powerful religious fervour. This hugely influenced the formation of numerous secret societies and thereafter the Swadeshi movement and the Agniyug. Ever since then, this heady cocktail of patriotism and Hindu religion has often turned more sectarian, while there has always been an attempt, less pronounced and comparatively weaker, to build a more sane and religion-free narrative.

***

A year later came the Ilbert bill. In those days, British subjects could not be tried by Indian magistrates, however grave their crimes may be. They often treated Indians with contempt and were ruthless. They were particularly merciless towards the downtrodden people like the indigo peasants, tea garden labourers and their domestic servants. Often there would be news of a British man having kicked or punched an Indian to death for some flimsy mistake. But the culprit would get away with minor punishment as the case was tried by his countryman. Such discrimination gave rise to huge resentment throughout the country.

To allay the people's disaffection, the Ilbert bill was mooted, named after C.P. Ilbert, the legal secretary of Governor-General Lord Ripon. The draft of the bill authorized senior Indian magistrates to try British subjects. As a natural consequence, the British subjects were furious at such a suggestion and all hell broke loose.

The white men were up in arms. They even insinuated that if this bill were to become a law, then the Indian magistrates would use their power to fill their harems with white women. The opposition to the bill was fierce. The response from the Indian educated class was lukewarm, though this discrimination caused them much heartburn.

The Indian Association failed to counter the British propaganda and disinformation. In the face of mounting pressure from their own countrymen, the government withdrew the bill; status quo was restored.

This humiliation caused some churning within the educated class that led to the formation of the Indian National Congress in 1885. But that's only a part of the story. The British, sensing that discontent was rising rapidly within the masses, which could burst into a rebellion, thought of an organization that would act as a safety valve to take the edge off people's grievances.

Allan Octavian Hume took the initiative of forming the organization with the help of Indian leaders and the tacit support of the government. The viceroy Lord Dufferin himself blessed the organization. Thus, the first session of the organization was held in Bombay from 28th to 31st December 1885. As expected, it expressed unequivocal allegiance to the British Raj.

But gradually, with the passage of time, people began to view the organization as their own, which could solve their problems, alleviate their sufferings. Year after year, its popularity began to rise. While in the first session of the party, the number of delegates was merely 72, in the fifth session held at Bombay, it rose to 1889.[15]

The British became concerned. The same Lord Dufferin began to treat the party with disdain, terming it an organization of miniscule minority. The government even decreed that if its employees attended the sessions of Congress even as a spectator, then it would be considered a cognizable offence. The Congress leadership turned out to be weak and spineless, and instead of taking on the government, they restricted themselves to petitions and supplications.

Amidst this insipidness, Bal Gangadhar Tilak of Puna rose like a meteor. He was a radical, stridently against the British. In 1893, he started Ganapati Utsav and Shibaji Utsav

---

15 Suprakash Roy, 1949. P. 31.

in the province of Bombay. He utilized the popularity of these festivals to propagate against the British.

Like many eminent personalities of those times, Tilak was fiercely anti-British, and at the same time, an orthodox, conservative Hindu. He vigorously opposed the British, being imprisoned several times. He also actively campaigned for cow-protection and was strongly opposed to the Age of Consent bill (raising the age of consent for sexual intercourse for all girls, married or unmarried, from ten to twelve) on the ground that it interfered with orthodox Hindu code.

In Bengal, it was Aurobindo Ghosh, later renowned as Rishi Aurobindo, who took up the task of rebuking the Congress for its mendicant policies. After returning from England in 1893, he severely criticized the Congress for having lost contact with the masses. More than a century and a quarter ago, he realized the importance of mass politics and called on the party to bridge the gap between the educated middle class and the common people. Curiously, at the same time, he advocated the worship of Ma Bhabani to seek her blessings for the liberation of the country. He advocated the building of a Bhabani mandir around which dedicated workers would be groomed, who like the 'santans' in *Anandamath* would be committed to the Mother and Motherland.

Swami Vivekananda also laid emphasis on developing physical strength. In a lecture at Madras in 1897, he said, "First of all, our young men must be strong. Religion will come afterwards. Be strong, my young friend; that is my advice to you. You will be nearer to heaven through football than through the study of the Gita."[16]

Yet at other occasions, he invoked Ma Kali, another avatar of the Mother Goddess, calling on young men to prepare themselves to rid the country of slavery, poverty and untouchability. Thus, time and again, we find that from its very inception, nationalism in India was heavily influenced by spiritualism, particularly Hindu dharma.

***

We have already seen that Jatin had a keen interest in outdoor activities. But he also read a lot. The night time sessions of childhood – when his mother read out passages from the epics, *Bhagavad Gita* or described the lives of great men – had created in him a lifelong yearning for knowledge. He had a peculiar fascination for the *Bhagavad Gita*.

When he was in the tenth standard at the Krishnanagar school, he scored the highest in physical exercises. He received three books as prize. These were *Gita*, *Anandamath* and *Shivaji Mahakabya* by Jogin Bosu.

Seeing the books, Jatin's uncle Basanta Kumar told him that of all the Hindu religious texts, *Gita* was supreme. He lectured him on *Gita*'s *Gyana yog, Karma yog* and *Bhakti yog*. While Jatin was not much interested in the strictly religious part, he wanted to model himself on Arjuna and become a dispassionate *Karma yogi*. He almost memorized some of

16 David M. Laushey, 1958.

Krishna's messages by which he inspired a despairing and battle-aversive Arjuna into action.

Later in life, when he came in contact with young revolutionaries, the first question he asked them was if they had read the *Gita*. If someone said he had not, he would promptly ask him not to come any longer. If someone questioned what relation does *Gita* have with fighting against the British, he would take him aside and make him realize that it was necessary to study the book to inspire oneself. Without inspiration, how would one fight against such a formidable enemy?

One afternoon, Jatin was just loitering through a bazaar at Krishnanagar. Suddenly, there was a commotion. People were running around in total confusion. Shopkeepers pulled down their shutters, pedestrians hid themselves wherever they could. Jatin saw a huge horse which had gone berserk and was running around wildly. People were scared and screaming in fear. Nobody dared approach the horse.

Jatin stood in the middle of the road, determined to take the beast head on. The people around beseeched him to flee, but he stood rooted to the spot, stretching out his bare hands. The wild animal perhaps annoyed at his audacity, charged at him with full speed and then suddenly stopped in front of him. This was the opportunity Jatin needed. He immediately caught hold of the beast by its mane. Neighing frantically, it raised its front legs and tried to straighten itself on its rear limbs. Jatin, with his immense strength, held it down and jumped onto its back. The horse desperately tried to shake Jatin off, but he held on firmly. He stroked its neck, caressed it, talked to it softly and the animal gradually came to its senses. When the horse seemed to have calmed down, its syce came running from behind a shop, fear still writ large on his face. It contrasted greatly with the smile on Jatin's face.

Everyone was surprised by this courageous feat of the teenager. His maternal uncles were proud of him. The distinguished people of the town and even the Raja of Krishnanagar praised him highly for acting so bravely in the face of imminent danger.

Back in Koya when his mother heard of this feat, she was reminded of the burning log that had helped her son chase the dog away. Perhaps that day, Jatin had chased away fear from his mind too. She was proud that her Jatin was growing up to be a fearless, upright man.

COMPASSIONATE, YET DEFIANT

In the year 1897, Jatin passed the entrance examination from his school in Krishnanagar. His uncles wanted him to complete his graduation and try for Indian Civil Service. They had the means to send him to London to study for ICS, and were committed to doing so. Sharatshashi, however, had other ideas.

As Jatin had completed his schooling, she wanted him to take up a job. Like traditional Bengali women, she felt uncomfortable living at her paternal house. She thought her family was being a burden on the brothers' families. Although she had been comfortable in the household, she harboured the wish to have her own house someday. Because of that, she wanted Jatin to become financially independent soon, so that they could go back to their own house at Jhinaidaha.

But Basanta Kumar put Sharat's worries to rest. He assured his sister that they were always at hand to care for her family; that it was their duty. Basanta was a wise man who had been observing the children of the household. With his keen eye, he knew that his nephew had a bright future. To ensure that Jatin's caliber could be honed to perfection, he was sent to his younger uncle, Hemanta Kumar, in Calcutta. Hemanta had wide connections. Eminent doctors Nilratan Sarkar and Suresh Sarbadhikari were his friends. Kshudiram Basu, the educationist, was also known to him. Basu had founded the Calcutta Central College at Hedua near College Street. Jatin was granted admission into this college. He lived at Hemanta's house, which was already full of students. Everyone from Koya and nearby villages had free access to this house and they were treated as well as Hemanta's own sons. They were not only assured of his uncle's shelter, but were also provided free food and clothing. Often, they took loans from the benevolent doctor, which some never cared to return. All his uncles had stellar qualities, which influenced him greatly and shaped his persona.

At about the same time as this, people were becoming more vociferous and beginning to protest against British exploitation. The subservient educated class was now becoming rebellious. Sporadic preparations for an armed resistance to imperialist rule began to take shape in far-flung Maharashtra. The province was then reeling under recurring famines and people were dying in thousands. Amidst this bleak scenario, Vasudev Balwant Phadke formed a secret society and launched occasional armed attacks on the British. With a ragtag band of hungry and impoverished roving rebels, he took on the might of the imperial forces.

As expected, it was an unequal battle and he was apprehended in 1879. He was sentenced to life imprisonment and died in jail in 1883. This became a process which continued unabated till India achieved independence. Dedicated young men and women would emerge in droves, who would sacrifice themselves at the altar of liberation of the motherland, only to be replaced by more such committed people, and the cycle would go on and on.

In 1896, there was a famine which severely affected United and Central provinces, and large parts of Bombay and Madras presidencies. At least one million people are said to have died. Bal Gangadhar Tilak began a 'no rent' campaign, thus beginning the process of involving the masses in the freedom movement. Invariably, the famine was followed by an epidemic. Bubonic plague spread to large parts of the Bombay province, particularly Puna.

The government took hard measures to combat the disease, often violating people's sentiments. They formed a special plague committee to control the epidemic. Its commander was Walter Charles Rand. Rand imposed restrictions ruthlessly. His officials and soldiers would often barge into homes and forage into people's belongings, defiling the sanctity of an orthodox Indian home. They also physically searched men and women, violating their modesty and even vandalized religious symbols.

Instead of combating the disease, they caused great offence to the people. The Chapekar brothers – Damodar Hari Chapekar, Balkrishna Hari Chapekar and Vasudeo Hari Chapekar – took up from where Phadke had left. The

Chapekars were brahmins by caste, very orthodox and religious. What the British officials were doing, was seen as an affront to their dharma. They decided to retaliate. To add salt to injury amidst this mayhem of deaths and disease, the diamond jubilee of Queen Victoria was celebrated with much pomp and revelry. On 22nd June 1897, Walter Charles Rand was shot by the Chapekar brothers, while he was returning from the celebrations. After the attack, his military escort Lieutenant Ayerst died on the spot, Rand succumbed to his injuries soon after.

The three Chapekar brothers were arrested and hanged to death. Tilak was charged with publishing incendiary articles in his newspaper, *Kesari*. What he, in fact, published was a poem named 'Shivaji's Utterances' and a report on Shibaji festival. Yet, the government claimed that he was spreading disaffection and sentenced him to eighteen months of rigorous imprisonment.

Tilak's supporters and others collected donations for fighting his case. Rabindranath Tagore himself took an active part in it. This created a bond between Maharashtra and Bengal, which proved to be fruitful in later years.

From Maharashtra, the movement spread to Bengal. Numerous societies sprouted up in west and east Bengal. In the beginning, these were not secret as such, though there were various kinds. There were the Congress volunteers who were mainly active during the sessions and conference of the party. There were others who were involved in social work. During natural calamities, famines and epidemics, they were always by the people – rescuing them, organizing food kitchens or medical camps. Lastly, there were the clubs and *samitis* which stressed on character building.

In these samitis, importance was given to mental and moral upbringing, for which it was mandatory to study religious texts and life of national and international heroes. They also tried to learn from the Irish struggle for independence and the Italian unification movement. But utmost importance was given on building physical power and strength. One had to go through rigorous physical exercises every day. Participants were taught various combat skills, like wrestling, fencing, lathi-khela, and even martial arts like jujutsu.

Often, the activities of the last two types of societies overlapped. When anti-British agitation intensified, some clubs went into secret mode. Experienced and more committed members of these clubs would form an inner core within the organization, making bombs or planning dacoities and attacks on the government. They would maintain a façade of open activities to hoodwink the police.

Jatin was mainly into social activities. After coming to Calcutta, he worked for the relief of cholera patients. In April 1898, an epidemic of plague broke out in the city. Around the same time, Sister Nivedita arrived, having been greatly influenced by Swami Vivekananda. She lived in a rented house at Baghbazar in north Calcutta. This indomitable Irish lady would have a great influence on Jatin. Nivedita straightway began relief work for the diseased.

Many students, including Jatin, followed her example. They were regularly seen cleaning and sanitizing city's streets. Nivedita was so moved by Jatin's dedication that she introduced him to Swami Vivekananda. The latter was very impressed with the striking young man. They had a brief but hearty conversation. Swamiji himself practiced wrestling and advised Jatin to learn the same at Ambu Guha's gymnasium. He also encouraged Jatin to continue with his social work.

Social activities came naturally to Jatin because this characteristic was imbibed in him from his family. All his maternal uncles were involved in various activities, wherever they lived. Jatin had grown up seeing them helping others, giving freely to whoever was in need and never saying no to the needy. This virtue of selfless service was imbibed in Jatin naturally.

At their family mansion at Koya, Durga Puja was celebrated with much grandeur every year. Village people participated in the festival en masse, irrespective of their caste or religion. Many respectable people of Kusthia and neighbouring places would take part in this congregation. An important ritual of the puja was the feasts laid out on all the four days of the festival.

Jatin and his young friends participated in every activity. They made huge mud *chullahs*[17] and cooked rice. They served the guests when they sat down to have their meal. In the afternoon, there would be sports. Jatin excelled in various activities like wrestling, rowing and, of course, horse-riding. Every evening, cultural festivities were held. Musical soirees and folk songs would be presented

17 Literally, mud stoves.

and troupes would often be hired from Krishnanagar and nearby towns. But the main attraction of the evening would be the Jatras, a form of theatre – unsophisticated, but hugely popular. Jatin was an enthusiastic participant and impressed everyone in the role of Maharana Pratap and Pratapaditya.[18]

Everyone who knew Jatin admired his multiple talents, and nobody had an iota of doubt that this young boy would reach great success. An ace horse rider, he was a swimmer par excellence, who was good at wrestling, speaking, lathi khela and other sports, and had a heart of gold. His dedication towards social work was exemplary. Sharat could see the astrologer's prediction coming true. Jatin would make her, the town, and the country, very proud.

Social work is an important facet of life. It makes people compassionate and sensitive to the needs of the distressed and downtrodden. Jatin was no exception. There are several incidents in his lifetime, when he helped those who were suffering or in dire need.

One day, he was returning from Kusthia. There happened to be a beggar on the boat. Jatin always made it a point to dress well, so the mendicant obviously thought that he was a wealthy man who could help him substantially.

"Baba, just see my clothes. Have pity on me... please help me," the poor man said and fell at Jatin's feet, sobbing.

Jatin swiftly stepped back and held him up by his shoulders. The man in front of him was barely a skeleton,

18 Uma Mukherjee, 2005. P. 171.

rags dangling over his body. He took out all the money he had in his pockets and handed it over to the man.

Jatin embraced him and told him lovingly, "You needn't wear old clothes. Buy some new ones for yourself."

There is another well-known incident highlighting his generosity. He was walking by the river ghat when he found a Muslim woman standing next to a huge bundle of grass. She was requesting every passerby to help her lift that bundle. She had to carry it home on her head, but couldn't pick it up alone. Nobody had time for her.

Jatin was moved by her plight and approached her. Finding someone so sympathetic, the poor woman poured her heart out to Jatin.

"I have a cow at home, and all this grass is for her," the woman said.

She again tried to raise the bundle up on her head, but it rolled over her shoulders. She had perhaps miscalculated how big and heavy it'd be for her. Already tired of trying to seek help, emotionally drained and anxious, she sighed and collapsed on the ground.

She lamented, "I requested so many people and they just walked past, not bothering to even listen to me."

Jatin promised to help her and lifted the load. He knew instantly that it was quite heavy and it'd be impossible for the frail woman to carry it home. She had told him she had to carry it for close to a mile. Jatin made his decision and picked up the load on his shoulders. Without once looking at the woman or the passerby who stopped in awe, he started walking. As usual, he was well dressed, and the muddy grass was wet. But Jatin didn't care about it and carried the bundle till the woman's house. On reaching her home, he also gave her some money. Needless to say, the woman was moved to tears.

In Calcutta, Jatin grew close to his youngest uncle Lalit Kumar. He was the son-in-law of Yogendra Bidyabhusan, an eminent thinker of the time and editor of a journal named *Aryadarshan*. Yogendra was not much interested in politics, but he wrote biographies of famous philosophers and revolutionaries to motivate the youth. Two of these were on Giuseppe Mazzini (1805-1872) and Giuseppe Garibaldi (1807-1882), heroes of the Italian unification movement. Lalit presented these two books to Jatin after he cleared an important examination.

Nivedita's home at Baghbazar became a veritable study centre for young men like Jatin. She had a good stock of books on various subjects. There were books on the Irish revolt, American independence, the revolt of 1857, and also books on firebrand revolutionaries like Mazzini and Garibaldi. She had books on economics also. These books were distributed to various secret societies, which were later discovered by the police at different hideouts.

For many of Jatin's generation, when repression and exploitation by the British was rising inexorably, the move from social work to armed revolutionary activity was an inevitable step. Jatin was very motivated by the life of Mazzini and asked everyone to read his biography to learn guerilla warfare.

However, duty to the nation had to be balanced with family responsibilities. Sharatshashi was growing more impatient by the day and wanted her son to take up a job instead of studying further. On the other hand, Basanta Kumar wanted Jatin to at least complete his B.A. Jatin was in a dilemma. He felt her mother's pain; he realized that his mother felt she and her children were being a burden on her brothers' family. But at the same time, Jatin knew that his uncles' love for him was genuine. They considered him as their own son.

Finally, Basanta relented and Jatin also felt that it was more important to make his mother smile than to build a career. He left college and began to learn shorthand and typing, which was a rare skill in those days. Within a few months, he became an expert steno-typist and went to various firms, hunting for a job. He didn't have any experience, nor did he have any recommendation. But he was so confident of his abilities that he sent applications to various companies and personally visited some offices.

Once he visited a merchant office at Dalhousie Square in the city. He looked handsome in his western attire. The Babu at the reception was very impressed and immediately fixed up his appointment with the *burra sahib*[19]. The sahib, a quintessential British, was rather amazed by Jatin's striking presence and his fluent English. He was immediately appointed, though the salary was not what Jatin had expected.

---

19 Literally, the big master/ senior.

After a few months, he landed a better job at Muzaffarpur, thanks to the connections of Lalit Kumar. While working at that remote town in Bihar, he received the news of his mother's illness. He rushed back to Koya and found his mother on her death bed. The village had again been hit by cholera and his mother was nursing her nephew when she got infected. She didn't recover, and at the young age of twenty, Jatin lost his mother.

Sharatshashi was the sun around which the lives of Jatin and Binodbala revolved. She was hugely influential in their character building. She was a hard taskmaster, yet she was tender, affectionate. All these qualities rubbed on her children as well and paved the way for their growth. Her sudden departure from their lives created a permanent void. Henceforth, Binodbala took over the role of a mother for Jatin.

***

The year after that, Jatin tied the knot with Indubala. It was his mother's ardent wish that her son marry Indubala, a girl she was very fond of. She was from Kumarkhali, a neighbouring village, and quite well-known to the Chatterjee family. They had a traditional married life with four children – Ashalata, Tobu, Tejendranath and Birendranath. We can get an inkling of their marital life from the only letter of Jatin to Indubala which survives. It was evidently written from Kaptipada where Jatin breathed his last, after a valiant gun fight with the British. Here is a glimpse into the contents of the letter:

> *We have been together for almost fifteen years and I have tried to convince you about the essence of humanity. I have tried to prepare you for the situation I am in at present. Take care of the children so that they become good human beings. Help Didi and consult her whcnever required. Remember, Purush or Man is only complete when it has Prakriti or Nature, arm-in-arm.*[20]

Even after he lost his mother, who had always been her anchor, he continued in his political activities. The fact that his mother had been nursing someone in her last days only instilled the feeling of sacrifice more.

Around the year 1901, Jatin is said to have started a revolutionary society at Koya.[21] F.C. Daly,[22] in his note on the 'Growth of the Revolutionary Movement in Bengal' states that one of the first secret societies to flourish was at Kushtia, in the Nadia district.

> *"This was organized by one Jotindra Nath Mukherjee, a clerk in the Financial Department in the Bengal Secretariat, who was subsequently arrested on a charge of planning the murder of the late Khan Bahadur Shamsul Khan."*[23]

Other accounts point out that he may have started similar societies in Krishnanagar as well.

---

20 Prithwindra Mukherjee, 2020. P.123.

21 Prof. Sumit Sarkar, 1994. P. 376.

22 Then DIG, Special Branch, Bengal.

23 Amalendu De, 2002. P. 104.

The attitude of the British towards the common men annoyed him greatly. They were arrogant, rude and quite often physically assaulted hapless Indians. Jatin didn't miss any opportunity to pay them back in their own coin.

Once, in a busy marketplace, a young boy inadvertently collided with a hawker. The chana from the hawker's cane basket lay strewn on the footpath. The hawker was beating the boy mercilessly, and nobody protested. Jatin interfered and paid the hawker one rupee – which was much more than the value of his entire stock back in those days. Jatin asked the hawker to let the boy go. The hawker threw away the rupee and said that he would not let the boy go until he was not paid at least five rupees.

That was too much for Jatin! In a fit of rage, he slapped the hawker. A British sahib was watching the incident. He sided with the chanawala and charged Jatin for bullying the hawker.

They argued, and it led to a fierce fight between Jatin and the white man. Jatin pinned his opponent down and forced him to apologize. He also held the terrified boy by his hand and took him home.

Another incident occurred at Gora Bazar near Fort William. The British tommies[24] residing in the barracks were very rude to the local shopkeepers. Jatin happened to be at the bazar for some errands one day. He saw a belligerent soldier hitting on the heads of the shopkeepers with his cane and counting – one, two, three... When he had counted up to 48, he found a stout young man standing in front of him.

---

24 Slang for a common soldier in the British army.

Jatin barked 49 and landed a fist on the soldier's face. The tommy fell flat and Jatin vanished in the crowd.

There are numerous such incidents when Jatin took on a highhanded white man. He wanted to prove that Bengalis were in no way inferior to the British. He could do it because he was strong and powerful. That is why societies like the Atmonnati Samiti formed in 1897 stressed on developing physical strength. This samiti was to play an important role during the agitation against the partition of Bengal. Jatin would be occasionally involved with this organization.

The year 1902 was remarkable; there were some momentous events, a heartbreaking one as well. Anushilan Samiti, the most important and arguably one of the most radical and progressive organizations that fought for India's independence was formed in this year. The word 'Anushilan' literally means 'repeated study or practice or training or cultivation'.[25] Its origin is in Bankim Chandra Chattopadhya's *Dharmattowo* and has profound religious and philosophical connotations. Roughly, it means that four impulses constitute a human being – physical, a craving for knowledge, the period of work or service, and aesthetic faculty of the mind. The joy, maturity and harmony of these four impulses define humanness. But we are putting the cart before the horse; the name was not decided at the outset, it came afterwards.

A number of factors spread over the last few years provided the spark that led to the formation of the

25 Samsad Bengali to English Dictionary.

organization. Aurobindo returned from England in 1893. He was already a firebrand, being a member of Lotus and Dagger Party, a secret society working for India's liberation in London.[26] He worked in the Congress to push through a more radical anti-British programme, at the same time working secretly for armed struggle.

After returning to India, Aurobindo took up work under the Gaekwads, the Maharaja of Baroda. Here he was initiated into the cult of revolutionary nationalism by one Thakur Saheb, who was a leader from Puna and very close to Tilak. He also became a member of a Gujarat based secret organization named Democratic India.[27] He realized that for starting an armed struggle, it was necessary for the youth to be properly trained. For this purpose, he inducted another Jatin, Jatin Bandyopadhyay into the armed forces of Baroda. Jatin Bandyopadhyay had a stint of military training. He occasionally came to Bengal, formed a secret group, and imparted training to young men.

At around the same time, Satish Chandra Basu, who was a student of General Assembly's Institution, which is presently the Scottish Church college, started a lathi-khela club at Madan Mitra lane. He came in contact with Pramatha Nath Mitra, famously known as P. Mitra, a reputed barrister, who – while studying in England – came to know about Irish and Russian revolutionaries. He had also learnt riding, boxing and fencing, and had tried to get into British army for military training. On his return to India, he met

---

26 Amalendu De, 2002. P. 22.

27 Buddhadev Bhattacharya, Niharranjan Ray, 1979. P-24.

Surendranath Banerjee and other Congress leaders. He did not approve of Congress' pacifist policies. He believed that India could only be freed by armed action, for which it was necessary to raise a band of fearless and dedicated men. At the same time, he advocated restraint and was against any rash, premature action. Nevertheless, he resolved to form a revolutionary group and kept in touch with various underground organizations.

At this point, two great friends of India, Sister Nivedita and Kazuko Okakura came into the picture. We have seen Nivedita, the social worker, but gradually, she would get involved in revolutionary activities as well, for which she was shunned by the Ramkrishna Mission during her last years. In the beginning of 1902, she went to Baroda and met Aurobindo. She apprised him about the situation in Bengal and also requested him to visit the province and bring the scattered societies together. Okakura was a proponent of Pan-Asianism and would later author the book *The Ideals of the East*. He too was fascinated by Swami Vivekananda's teachings. He invited Swamiji to visit Japan, which he could not, due to his poor health. Okakura came to Calcutta in late 1901 and met P. Mitra, Nivedita, Sarala Devi Chaudhurani (niece of Rabindranath Tagore) and other important personalities. He expressed surprise that India having such an ancient past and great civilisation was enslaved by the British. He impressed upon the audience that Asia with its great heritage was superior to the West. The involvement of these two 'Bharat-Bandhu'[28] proved crucial.

28 Literally, friends and well wishers of India.

On 24th March 1902, the day of Doljatra and full moon, Anushilan Samiti was formed at Madan Mitra Lane near Hedua in Calcutta. Later, its office was shifted to Cornwallis Street, presently known as Bidhan Sarani. A central committee of the organization was formed – P. Mitra was the President; Aurobindo Ghosh and Chittaranjan Das, another famous barrister who later left Congress and formed the Swaraj party, were the Vice-Presidents; and Surendranath Thakur was the Treasurer. The headmaster of New Indian School, Narendra Chandra Bhattacharya, named the society Bharat Anushilan Samiti. Later, P. Mitra trimmed it to Anushilan Samiti.[29]

In the middle of 1905, during Pratapaditya Utsab, Ashutosh Ghosh, a distinguished educationist of the Khidderpur branch of the Samiti first raised the slogan of *Bande Mataram*. It spread like a raging flame and became a clarion call for all anti-British agitations throughout the nation. It still continues to motivate vast sections of the Indian society.[30]

Just four months later, on 4th July, Swami Vivekananda passed away. He was only thirty-nine years old. He was not merely a religious thinker. His ideas on upliftment of the downtrodden and eradication of untouchability mark him as an important social reformer of the time. His untimely death shocked the beleaguered nation reeling under imperialist repression. Jatin was heartbroken. Swamiji was his idol; he literally emulated the venerable sage.

---

29 Jibantara Halder, P. 29-30.

30 Ibid, P. 33.

A FIREBRAND IN HER MAJESTY'S SERVICE

After returning from Muzaffarpur on hearing about his mother's illness, Jatin had not gone back to his old job. Instead, he worked at a merchant office in the city, named Ahmutty & Co. Later, he got a better opportunity with a higher pay. Subsequently, on 11th August 1903, he was appointed as a typist at the Bengal Secretariat. On 15th May 1904, he was appointed stenographer to the Financial Secretary to the Government of Bengal on a monthly salary of one hundred rupees. He worked directly under Henry Wheeler, who was then a very influential man, in charge of many government activities in the Bengal province.

Since Jatin was his steno-typist, he had direct access to Wheeler. The latter also liked Jatin for his efficiency and amiable behaviour. Being in charge of revenue, many rajas and landlords would come to visit Wheeler. That's how Jatin became acquainted with many prominent persons of the time. This *sarkari* job worked as a good masquerade for Jatin's political activities, for who would suspect a man who was employed under one of the foremost functionaries in the government!

In the same year, he secretly met Aurobindo and Jatin Bandopadhyay at the residence of Jogendra Nath Vidyabhusan at Shyampukur Street, Calcutta. It was from these two stalwarts that he received his baptism in the nation's freedom struggle. In fact, Jatin organized "a branch of the Anushilan in far off Darjeeling, while serving there as a finance department clerk." This is "virtually the only known instance of swadeshi activity in this outlying northern district of Bengal, whose hill peoples remained indifferent towards the agitation, despite a few early attempts at political speeches in Nepali."[31]

According to police reports in 1907, Jatin had been sent to Darjeeling on some special work. "From early youth, he had the reputation of a local Sandow and he soon attracted attention in Darjeeling in cases in which, true to his reputation as one of the earliest exponents of the physical force party, he tried to measure his strength with Europeans. In 1908, he was the leader of one of the several gangs that had sprang up in Darjeeling, whose object was the spreading of disaffection, and with his associates he started a branch of the Anushilan Samiti, called the Bandhab Samiti.[32]

After its formation, Anushilan Samiti began to open branches in various localities of Calcutta. It also spread to the suburbs and villages. The central committee used to send teachers to the branches. Physical exercises, lathi-khela and

---

31 Sumit Sarkar, 1994. P. 376.

32 Uma Mukherjee, 2005. P. 174.

fencing were taught. Dagger-wielding, boxing and jujutsu were also practiced. There were often mock fights, military drills and mock capture of forts or garrisons. Rowing and horse-riding were practiced. Swimming competitions were held in the Ganges. There were sports like *kabaddi* and *ha-du-du*, a similar version of the former. For improving the physique, sit-ups and push-ups were done. Wrestling was very popular, though lathi-khela was more popular.

P. Mitra himself was attracted to it from his very childhood. He was an expert in wielding the lathi and practiced regularly with his friends. He was so fascinated by the sport that he even wrote an essay on it in the magazine *Bengalee,* edited by Surendranath Banerjee. He wrote:

> *"The lathi is the national weapon of Bengal. A Bengalee lathial, properly trained, can with his single lathi keep half dozen swordsmen at bay."*

The article goes on to elaborate and exalt the various qualities and advantages of lathi-khela and concludes that, "we should be unwise if we allow it to die away from our midst."

Along with harnessing physical strength of the participants, equal importance was given to mental, moral and spiritual development as well. Books like *Maharashtra Jiban Probhat, Annals and Antiquities of Rajasthan* by James Todd, and books on French revolution, Russian nihilism, the revolt of 1857, Mazzini, Garibaldi and Indian heroes were studied. The Samiti had a library of more than four thousand books, many of which had been donated by Sister Nivedita.

Discussions were held on politics, economics and the socio-political condition of the country. Students were taken on educational visits to places like the residence of Swami Vivekananda, Bankim Chandra, well-known poet Michael Madhusudan Dutt, Belur Math, etc.

For spiritual development, *Gita, Ramayana, Mahabharat* and even *Vedas* and *Upanishad* were read and discussed. Study material for spiritual development consisted almost entirely of Hindu religious texts. This made the Samiti a primarily Hindu organization. Some members occasionally objected to this. For instance, Bhupendranath Dutta, Swami Vivekananda's younger brother, refused to take vows on Hindu Shastras only. Hemchandra Kanungo was vocal against mixing patriotism with religion. Khagendranath Das complained that the stress on adhering to Hindu rituals was alienating the Brahmos and the Muslims. There continued to be objections to these practices even later. This over emphasis on the majority religion proved to be a serious weakness of the organization.

Despite all these small challenges, spirits used to be high, almost electric, and every session used to end with full-throated and enthusiastic singing of *Bande Mataram*. Suffice to say that at least in the initial stages, there was nothing subversive, conspiratorial or revolutionary about the Samiti's activities. The British were cautious, but hardly concerned.

But stormy clouds were gathering in the sky, particularly in Bengal. The proposal of bifurcation of the province was in the air. Initially the reason put forward for breaking up the province was because it was huge and unmanageable. Bengal Presidency then included, apart from proper Bengal, east and west Bihar, Orissa, Assam and the whole of northeast. It covered an area of 1,89,000 miles and had a whopping population of 78.5 million. The idea was first mooted after the 1866 famine in Orissa, during which 4 to 5 million people were reported to have died. During the same period, 200 million pounds of rice were exported to Britain, due to which the nationalists obviously raised the 'drain theory' and alleged that the disaster was manmade.

However, according to the government, the calamity had occurred because of the enormous size of the province, which made the then remote region of Orissa ungovernable. In 1874, Assam was separated and it set the ball rolling. In 1892, a proposal to amalgamate south Lusai hills (now known as Mizoram) with Assam was mooted. Another proposal was that the entire Chittagong division, including the Chittagong hills, Noakhali and Tippera (now Tripura), should also go with it. Another idea was to add Dacca and Mymensingh as well, making Assam a full-fledged administrative unit. After all these discussions, for the time being, only south Lusai hills merged with Assam and there was a lull in the process for a few years.

Around 1902, readjustment of boundaries again came up for discussion due to the problem of Sambalpur, an Odia speaking area lying in the Central Provinces, which is predominantly Hindi-speaking. Elsewhere in India, reshaping various provinces was high on the government agenda. The next year, the addition of Chittagong hills,

Dacca and Mymensingh into the new province again came up in bureaucratic discussions. As it had been proposed a decade back, more areas were included subsequently to make Assam a full-fledged province.

In 1904, George Curzon[33] went on a tour of East Bengal and promised an expansion of the new province. It was not an empty promise. From April to September of the same year, more districts were added to the proposed new province, including parts of North Bengal. On 2nd February 1905, Curzon sent the final scheme to the Secretary of State. On 19th July, government announced the formation of a new province, curving out large chunks of Bengal and attaching it with Assam. This new province was named 'Eastern Bengal and Assam' and included, besides Assam, the whole of present Bangladesh, Tippera hills and Malda district. Formal proclamation of formation of this new province was made on 1st September and Bengal was finally partitioned on 16th October 1905.

Whatever the excuses government gave, it was clear that 'Divide and Rule' was the colonialists' primary motive behind the bifurcation. They knew that given the current scenario, that was the only way they could rule a vast and diverse country like India. So needless to say, cut and paste of provinces was not merely an administrative affair. It was not merely because provinces were large that they were being cut and chopped. The British were a cunning lot; their motive was not to let any nationality unite. Their aim was to

33 Viceroy of India from 1899 to 1905.

separate them into different geographical units, preferably on religious lines. They didn't want Marathas or Bengalis, or for that matter any nationality, to be in a single province.

As early as the last decade of nineteenth century, a proposal had come up to curve out a predominantly Muslim province out of Bengal. They felt that the power of the educated Hindu community could be curtailed in that way. Andrew Fraser, who became Lieutenant Governor of Bengal in 1903, felt that cutting of those eastern districts, which were politically volatile, would reduce the burden and hassle of governing Bengal. Herbert Risley, a colonial administrator, was more direct about his views. He felt, "Bengal united is power; Bengal divided will pull in several different ways." He further clarified, "...our main object is to split up and thereby weaken a solid body of our opponents to our rule."

Needless to say, this 'solid body of our opponents' is the educated Hindu community, vibrant with the rising tide of nationalism. They wanted to clip the wings of the talkative and audacious Bengali Babus, "who like to think themselves a nation, and who dream of a future when the English will have been turned out and a Bengali Babu will be installed in Government house in Calcutta."[34]

Finally, Curzon in his speech in Dacca on 18th February 1904 made the government's intention crystal clear, if any further clarifications were needed. He declared that the scheme "would invest the Mohammedans in Eastern Bengal

---

34 Sumit Sarkar, 1994. P. 418.

with a unity they have not enjoyed since the days of the old Mussulman viceroys and kings..."[35]

From as early as 1903, privileged sections of the society were aware that the bifurcation of the province was imminent. In anticipation of the people's response, Curzon had jokingly remarked that "they will slay me in Bengal." The bureaucrats were quite certain that after certain rumblings and grumblings, the natives will adjust to the new arrangements. They were right to an extent as the initial response was undoubtedly lukewarm. It followed the beaten track of letters, petitions, pamphlets, memorandum to the government, the typical Congress path of mendicancy.

In hindsight, it is clear that it could not have been otherwise as the initial response came from the privileged class – the zamindars, lawyers, merchants, petty bureaucrats, politicians, etc. They resented the fact that their area of influence had been squeezed, and so were their privileges. But their opposition had little popular support. It is interesting to find that the various pamphlets they issued during the period contained little on rousing the people and embarking on an agitation against partition. These were mere pleas to the English public, fervent appeals to their so-called good sense. Naturally, such staid opposition was unable to stop the partition.

Rabindranath himself cautioned that it would be unwise to depend on the benevolence of the rulers. Bipin Chandra Pal, considered an extremist in the Congress, remarked

---

35 Sumit Sarkar, 1994. P. 376.

famously that the failure to stop the partition proved the futility of the constitutional path of political agitation.

The Anushilan Samiti also could not put up any resistance to the partition of the province. It was facing its own organizational problems almost from its very inception. Within a few months of its formation, Barindra Kumar Ghosh, Aurobindo Ghosh's brother, who was at Baroda, came to Calcutta. He was sent by Aurobindo himself to support Jatin Bandyopadhyay, to help him to organize and spread the Samiti's activities. He went around Bengal for almost two years, trying to arouse the youth. Ostensibly, he failed to extract any significant response; instead, he got involved in a personal feud with Jatin Bandyopadhyay.

Jatin was a strict disciplinarian, which Barindra abhorred. He detested his leadership. In fact, he detested anyone's leadership. He used to brag that he had not come to the world to follow others, but that he himself was a leader whom others would follow. He cooked up derogatory charges against Jatin, alleging that he was involved in an illicit affair with a woman. Hereafter there are several versions of this episode. It is said that Aurobindo himself enquired and found that the charges were baseless. He tried to patch up their differences. Other accounts say that Aurobindo had egged on his brother against Jatin. Whatever the actual events may have been at that time, Jatin was disillusioned and left the organization. He became a sadhu and came to be known as Swami Niralamba. This was a setback for the organization for Jatin was an excellent organizer and had helped immensely in spreading the Samiti. Thus, Barin

Ghosh pioneered the culture of groupism or forming cliques and coteries within a party, which has remained the bane of Bengal politics to this day.

Jatindranath Mukherjee, the protagonist of our narrative, held both Aurobindo and Jatin Bandyopadhyay in high esteem. We have seen earlier how he was baptized into the cult by these two pioneers of the Anushilan Samiti. Now, when differences cropped up between the two, it was difficult for him to take sides. Jadugopal Mukhopadhyay, one of the many ardent followers of Jatin who addressed him as Dada, writes in his book *Biplobi Jiboner Smriti* that he had no idea if Dada belonged to any particular group. But he was sure that Jatin was not a member of Anushilan. Jatin certainly was not the type to indulge in any groupism; he was a character who remained above this petty-mindedness. Even then it's on record that Barin disliked him, so much so that he tried to test his commitment to the cause. In 1907, he sent Prafulla Chaki, a young man barely out of his teens, to Jatin, who was then in Darjeeling. Prafulla sought the help of Jatin to assassinate Lieutenant Governor Fraser. Jatin brushed his plea aside. Time is not ripe for such an action, he chided the young man. At the same time, he promised to help him in the future. Barin, on hearing this, had caustically remarked, "What more can you expect from a government servant!" What's more, Barin detested anyone who frequented Jatin.[36]

Due to these internecine problems, the revolutionary movement was then in a crisis. Partition of the province

---

36 Prithwindra Mukherjee, 2020. P. 46-47.

provided this disunited lot an issue to bury their differences. An external factor proved to be literally a godsend. Russia and Japan went to war on 4th February 1904. Everyone thought it would be a David vs Goliath affair. But the valour of the Japanese stunned the world. The way they fought the mighty Russians gladdened all of Asia. The 'firingis' or the whites are not invincible, people suddenly realized. And if tiny Japan can, then why can't we, a country of two hundred and forty millions, throw the British out from our country?

There was a sudden spark in the anti-partition agitation. Jatin and Amarendra Chatterjee helped to set up Chhatra Bhandar in Calcutta, a secret society centre masquerading as general stores. There were protest meetings, leafleting, pamphleteering glorifying the Japanese and exhorting the people to mobilize in protest against the colonialists. Bhupendranath Dutta excelled in oratory skills and Debabrata Bose lent him good support. The movement spread to districts like Nadia and Medinipur. Satyen Bose, nephew of Rajnarayan Bose, expanded the organization in Medinipur district. This was the time when the celebrated martyr Kshudiram Bose, the frail yet bright and vibrant teenager, joined the movement.

At the fag end of 1905, the Prince of Wales visited Calcutta in an attempt to appease the people's anger over the bifurcation of the province. Jatin was present at the spot by which the Royalty's cavalcade passed. A carriage stood in the side lane in which there were ladies who had come to witness the show. British soldiers sat on top of the carriage, dangling their feet in front of the windows behind which the ladies sat. Their language was filthy, their attitude boorish. Jatin protested. They ridiculed him. Jatin instantly jumped up on the carriage and pulled down the soldiers, giving them a good thrashing. The crowd howled in approval. The incident didn't go unnoticed by the dignitary. On returning to London, he spoke at length with John Morley, the Secretary of State, and expressed his displeasure at the behavior of the soldiers.

Just after the visit of the prince, Calcutta and various parts of Bengal were caught up in an epidemic of cholera. Tragically, Jatin's dear son Tobu, only two years old, succumbed to the disease. Jatin was devastated. Nothing could console him. He wandered around listlessly, oblivious of whatever was happening around him. Nothing in life seemed to matter anymore. Who could console him? How could the pain of losing a son be subdued? This search took him to the Himalayas, where he searched the ghats and the ashrams for someone who could soothe his bereaved soul.

He had come to know about Guru Bholanand Giri, a revered sanyasi who often came to Calcutta. He had many disciples in the city, and Hemanta Kumar was one of them. His abode was situated at Haridwar, on the bank of the Ganges. The serenity of the ashram had an instantly calming effect on Jatin. Giri Maharaj was considered a *mahayogi*, a *mahapurush* and very well known among the *sadhus*.

"*Kya hua beta*? What is the matter? You are not one to brood!" Maharaj was surprised when Jatin went to see him. "I understand your loss." He shook his head and looked up at the sky.

There was silence, heavy with unspoken words. A cold breeze blew from the mountains looming far away. The river gurgled, a hum of the pilgrims' activities was faintly audible.

"I understand your loss," the sanyasi repeated. "But you can't brood." He looked straight at Jatin, his eyes like burning coal. "Greater responsibilities await you in life."

The Maharaj stood up, took Jatin by his arm. Together they walked towards the river, towards the melee of early morning bathers. Maharaj gesticulated and went on speaking to him. They sat on the ghat and went on talking, even when the sun was up and it was hot. This long interaction seemed to have transformed Jatin. When he came back to the ashram, he had a different look on his face, as if he was in a trance. He returned home fresh and contented, ready to embark on a difficult journey.

By then, the movement against the bifurcation of the state had picked up. The sudden spurt in the movement encouraged Aurobindo to start a weekly newspaper. It was called *Jugantar,* named after a novel by Shibnath Shastri, a renowned scholar and social activist of the era. On 12th March 1906, the first edition of the paper was published. Significantly, the emblem of this paper had the symbols of both the Hindu and Muslim communities – the Trishul and Chakra of Hindu dharma and the crescent and sword of Islam.

Jugantar turned out to be quite distinct in the sense that it tried to forge Hindu-Muslim unity and bury religious differences. At least an effort was started to foster social and religious harmony. Unity in diversity – that is the hallmark of Bharatvarsha, the paper said. There have been many communities in India, but none have been harassed for following their faith. Various communities like Jews, Parsees, Muslims, Christians have made India their home, but this land has never denied them their place. This magnanimity has made our country a melting pot of different faiths, such was the lofty ideal of the paper.[37]

Jugantar focused on anti-British propaganda and openly called for a revolt against the tyrannical colonialists. The paper fearlessly encouraged discussions on strikes and rebellious activities in Russia and America. They even encouraged debates on Marx's ideas on strikes, *bandhs* and *hartals*. That workers had a legitimate right to strike was first found in this paper. By highlighting the working class movements in various nations, *Jugantar* espoused the concept of 'internationalism', a lofty idea unheard of in India ever before.

The publication of *Jugantar* was a definite boost for the Anushilan Samiti. At the same time, a coterie of young members began to form around the paper. For quite a while, this group led by Barin had been demanding more action from the leadership. They were not satisfied with mere lathi-khela, fencing, wrestling, moral lectures, etc. They wanted direct action against the British. P. Mitra didn't agree. He favoured a more moderate, restrained approach. He advocated patience. He felt the time was not yet ripe for

---

37 Amalendu De, 2002. P. 27-28.

any daring action; it would be rash, sheer adventurism. The differences remained unresolved.

Some months later, an All Bengal Revolutionary Conference was held at a house in what was then the Wellington Square in Calcutta. Representatives of almost all important societies from various districts were present in the conference. Here, an effort was made to patch up the differences between the elderly leadership and the young brigade. P. Mitra presided and demanded absolute obedience from everyone present. On his part, he urged the participants to extend their support to *Jugantar*, to increase its circulation and spread it far and wide. However, this unity was superficial and short-lived. We will find that within a year, the young brigade literally hijacked the organization and a culture of bomb and violence came to prevail.

It was a month after the launch of *Jugantar* that an incident occurred in Jatin's life, that gave him the celebrated and endearing sobriquet Bagha Jatin. He was on a holiday at his village Koya. One day, early in the morning, some villagers came running to the Chatterjees' residence. They were excited and frightened.

"Dada, bagh!" They exclaimed. Their faces were pale, eyes were fearful. It was learnt that a tiger was on the prowl in the village.

"It's taking away our livestock. Anything can happen... Please do something," the villagers beseeched Jatin.

"Please come with your gun, Dada," they folded their hands and kneeled down in the courtyard.

The Chatterjees were affluent; everyone knew the family had guns in the house. Unfortunately, it was an out-dated firearm. But undaunted, Jatin picked up the *khukri*[38] which he had brought from Darjeeling, and ran to the spot. His cousin followed him with the gun.

A crowd had gathered there, most of them beating canisters, trying to bring the animal out of hiding, into the open. Jatin saw a bush of tall grass swaying. He tiptoed up to it and tried to peer through the foliage. Suddenly, out of nowhere, the terrifying beast jumped at him. His cousin panicked and fired, but the bullet grazed the animal's skin.

Furious, the tiger flattened Jatin on the ground. But even under the immense weight of the tiger and the situation, he didn't lose his common sense. He repeatedly thrust the khukri into the tiger. Man and animal rolled on the ground, locked in a fatal embrace. Jatin called out to his cousin to fire, but how could he! The bullet could hit Jatin himself. It was a titanic struggle.

Jatin' body was scarred by scratches. Blood flowed, and the tiger's thunderous howls rent the air. Mustering all his strength, Jatin threw off the massive body and somehow stood up staggering. The tiger pounced back, attacking Jatin's thigh muscles. Jatin finally struck the khukri into its neck, which proved fatal. The beast lay sprawled on the ground and Jatin collapsed on it.

Many thought it was the end, as Jatin was bleeding profusely. He was rushed to Calcutta. Hemanta Kumar himself was a doctor, but even then, he preferred to call

---

38 A curved steel knife with a sharp edge; a type of machete.

Dr Sureshchandra Sarbadhikary, a renowned surgeon. Initially many thought that both his legs would have to be amputated. But the doctor put all his expertise to treat this brave young man.

As Jatin was being taken to the operation room, he opened his eyes and said with a faint smile, "Doctor, you don't have to anaesthetize me. Let me be in my senses; I can bear it."

The doctor was amazed. Here was a man, almost on the verge of death, and yet he was asking to be treated without anaesthesia!

He believed this man was the pride of the nation and curing him would be his real prize as a physician. He was so concerned about Jatin's treatment that he himself came to dress his wounds every single day.

In about two months, Jatin recovered, walking with a stick for some days. As a mark of gratitude, he presented the skin of the striped tiger to Dr Sarbadhikary. It was laid on the floor of the Doctor's house for years thereafter.[39]

The news of Jatin's daring exploit spread far and wide. He became famous as the man who *slayed a tiger with a bare dagger*.

Jadugopal in his book fondly reminisces how he first came to know him. He was simply in awe of him as we find in his memoirs:

> *Now let me tell you in brief how I came to know Jatindranath. My father had bashed up a firingi at the*

39 Ume Mukherjee, 2005. P. 176.

young age of eighteen. My youngest uncle Gourbabu had fought with a tiger. I considered myself fortunate for the same. But after some time, pride gave away to melancholy. I felt heroes were born before, but no longer now. Just then in 1906 the incident of a young man killing a tiger barely with a khukri came out in the newspaper. My pride was boundless because I belonged to an era of heroes. When he came to Calcutta, I looked at him with eyes brimming with admiration. His name was Jatindranath Mukherjee. He is my 'Surbir', hence a feeling of kinship engulfed me. I waited to know his thoughts, ideals, principles, his likes and dislikes. Then the government created such an opportunity. Intentionally I never met him face-to-face. I used to hear about him from friends, particularly from Narendranath Bhattacharya. My first interaction with him was on 12th February 1915, after the Garden Reach dacoity.

(Narendranath Bhattacharya later became famous as M.N. Roy. He became a Communist and then a Radical Humanist. Jadugopal was a dedicated revolutionary who was fortunate to be a witness to the entire freedom movement. He was born in 1886 and passed away in 1976. Both of them were very close to Jatin).

It took Jatin almost two months to recover from his injuries. But then, how could he sit idle at home! It was the time when the Swadeshi *andolon* and boycott of foreign goods was picking up. Earlier, Surendranath Banerjee had toured the country exhorting the people to boycott Manchester clothes and Liverpool salt. Even common people joined the movement in huge numbers. Foreign goods were boycotted. Dhobis refused to wash foreign clothes, cobblers refused to mend foreign shoes. If any neighbour used Liverpool salt, then that family was socially boycotted.

In one year, from 1904 to 1905, the import of foreign clothes to Bengal had decreased by 75%, the import of foreign shoes had decreased by 50%, and foreign salt by 80%. In this way, import of all foreign goods came down drastically.[40] On the other hand, there was a craze for Swadeshi, homegrown goods. *Atmashakti, Atmanirbhor* – self-sustenance – were the call of the times. As a result, swadeshi textile mills, matchsticks, soap factories, improved handlooms, tanneries came up. Melas and huts, rural fairs and bazaars were encouraged to sell local products.

Rabindranath Tagore stressed on *gram samaj,* an autonomous rural society. British business was hit hard. Bengal and its people became a nightmare for the mighty British. Rarely had passive resistance achieved such huge popularity and success. Referring to the movement against Bengal's bifurcation, Mahatma Gandhi said in 1908 that, "Bangabhanga brought about real renaissance in India... this will lead to the break-up of the British empire. After Bangabhanga, people came to realize that for a movement to succeed, they have to be firm and resolute and have to withstand pain and suffering.[41]

---

40 Tarapada Lahiri, 2005. Pp. 74, 88.

41 Ibid, P-74.

Opposing western education was another important aspect of the movement. Samitis and clubs started using Bengali language for political propaganda. The government response was harsh. Robert Warrand Carlyle, Chief Secretary of Bengal, issued a circular on 22nd October 1905, which stated that, "if any college violates the government order and the student quits the educational institution, then no assistance will be provided by the government to the institution."

This added fuel to the fire. National College of Bengal was established to encourage learning in the mother tongue. An Anti-Circular group came up overnight. It was very distinct from other samitis as it was strictly opposed to any form of Hindu revivalism. The group had many Muslim volunteers. It fostered religious amity and helped in stopping riots in some places.

Amidst this, Lokmanya Tilak arrived in the city in June, 1906 to celebrate Shibaji Utsav. He was very popular and was given a huge welcome in the city. The firebrand leader's presence made the festival special, and was celebrated with much resolve and gaiety. Tales of Shibaji's valour motivated the youth. They attended the occasion in huge numbers. Young men and women exhibited physical exercises, lathi-khela and fencing. An idol of the Maratha king with a sword by his side adorned the arena. There was also an idol of Bhawani. Anti-circularists objected to this blatant show of religious passion, but their objection was brushed aside.

Tilak declared, "We all are Hindus and idolators and I am not ashamed of the fact…we cannot conceive of Shibaji without Bhawani."[42]

Religion held sway over reason and everyone offered puja to the king's sword. Government employees stayed away, lest they incur the wrath of the authorities. But Jatin, true to his character, didn't care and offered puja with red china roses. Rabindranath composed the famous poem *Shivaji Utsav* for the occasion. Here is a stanza from that poem:

> No one had imagined in these three centuries
> Nor dreamt in their sleep
> That your hallowed name one day, without battle
> Would unite Bengal and Maratha.
> The power of your penance, long curtailed in oblivion
> Abruptly, today
> Like an everlasting message, would instill a fresh new life
> Upon a fresh new dawn![43]

42 Sumit Sarkar, 1994. P. 422.

43 Translated by Dr. Monish R Chatterjee, Professor at the University of Dayton.

A LIFE OF BOMBS, GUNS AND VIOLENCE

The first Lieutenant Governor of the new province of 'Eastern Bengal and Assam' was Bampfylde Fuller. He was a snob, contemptuous of the natives. He always demanded respect, he demanded a salam or a bow. He took great pride and delight in seeing terrified people running helter skelter when he was riding by on a horse, or passing by in a cavalcade. He was a typical colonial administrator – tough, even draconian. He banned the chanting of *Bande Mataram* at many places, his police withheld permission to hold several swadeshi meetings. But the brutal way in which his administration came down on a meeting held in Barisal was unprecedented.

A conference was held in this town in eastern Bengal in April, 1906. All shades of political opinion then existing in both the old and the new province were represented in this conference. The province was already in the iron-grip of Fuller's rule. The leaders and delegates began to arrive from 13th April. At the very outset, they were told that sloganeering of Bande Mataram was prohibited. Everyone decided to flout the order and proceeded to their destination on foot. Many proudly flaunted the Bande Mataram badge on their chest. Though there was no slogan-shouting, the police obstructed the procession and began a brutal lathi-charge. The onslaught so enraged the participants that they began to shout Bande Mataram. The harder the police brought down their lathis, the greater became the resistance, and thunderous slogans rent the air. Surendranath went up to the police officers and asked them to arrest him and stop beating the processionists. He was taken to the district magistrate and treated with utter disrespect. When he returned to the conference hall, he was greeted with loud shouts of Bande Mataram.

Thereafter, the first day's business was conducted peacefully and everyone thought the problem was over. But the next day, prohibitory orders were enforced and the participants were not even allowed to gather for the meeting. As a result, the conference had to be called off.[44]

This was a severe blow to the prestige and credibility of the moderate section of the leadership. The radicals sharpened their knives and reiterated that for a long time they had been clamouring for abandonment of the policy of appeasement and advocating radical action. This Barisal Conference proved to be the turning point in the revolutionary politics of Bengal. It became clear that moderate politics was helpless in the face of the draconian measures of the government.

---

44 Buddhadeva Bhattacharyya, 1979. Pp. 37-39.

Subsequently, the Congress session in Surat was an ugly affair, where the moderate and extremist factions literally came to blows. The split between the two camps, which was always apparent, now became clear and almost unbridgeable. Only twenty-two years after its formation, Congress was literally on its death throes. Barin and company was elated. Barin's reactions regarding the delegates from other states was rather deplorable. He even declared that everyone there was a *chor,* or at best, arm-chair politicians. "We will chart our own way," he declared. The bomb was the answer. And so, Bengal's destiny took a different route.

Jatin was recuperating from the injuries he had suffered in the encounter with the tiger. As a result, he could not attend the Barisal Conference. He was then transferred to Darjeeling and thus left out of tumultuous events that occurred in the state. The young brigade of *Jugantar* gradually became uncontrollable and P. Mitra became a mere spectator in the Anushilan Samiti. On 6th June 1906, *Jugantar* carried an article which exhorted the people to "rise in war or revolt" against the foreign rule, "if even fifty millions of man disappeared from India in an attempt at deliverance."

Another revolutionary newspaper named *Bande Mataram* was founded by Bipin Chandra Pal in 1905, and edited by Aurobindo. But the most strident paper was *Sandhya,* edited by Brahmabandhab Upadhyay. It spewed venom against the rulers and became very popular.

"Abundant supplies should be laid in of... that *Kali Ma's boma*" (the bombs of goddess Kali), one article said. Another called on the people, "arm brothers, arm! The day of deliverance is near."[45]

These inflammatory articles spurred on the young men. Bombs and guns henceforth became the main political agenda. A rudimentary bomb-making workshop had already been put up at a house belonging to Barin's family at Manicktala, then a suburb of Calcutta. Jatin initially frequented this place but didn't get too involved. His idea of combating the British was by guerilla struggle or insurrection, though later he had no option but to indulge in individual killings and dacoities.

A motley group of boys worked there with paltry tools. They lived a frugal life, but they dreamed big – to liberate the country in ten-fifteen years. Bombs were tried out in the hills of Deoghar, a town in today's Jharkhand, nearly three hundred and fifty kilometres away from the city. Jatin visited the place a couple of times, more out of curiosity than any other purpose. A bright young man perished there one day, when a bomb exploded accidentally. But that proved to be a minor hiccup and the preparations continued with as much enthusiasm as before.

The first attempt was made on Bampfylde Fuller, the villain of Barisal. Ostensibly, Bengali Bhadralok leaders were so enraged by the governor's action that they were ready to pay cash to ensure his death. Barin, along with Hemchandra Kanungo and Prafulla, chased him with homemade bombs

45 Buddhadeva Bhattacharyya, 1979. P. 42-43.

from Shillong to Barisal to Rangpur and lastly to Naihati.[46] Finally, a bomb was placed on the track at Naihati railway station, but Fuller's train took a different route. Next, an attempt was made on Governor Fraser near Narayangarh. Dynamites were placed on the railway tracks. The train was derailed and governor's compartment damaged, but he escaped unhurt. A former district magistrate of Dacca, Mr. Allen was shot on the back at a railway station of Faridpur district in Eastern Bengal. He was saved by immediate medical treatment. There was an attempt on Tardivelle, the French Mayor of Chandannagar, but this also proved to be abortive.

Douglas H. Kingsford, magistrate of Calcutta, became the next target. He was so inhuman towards young freedom fighters that it enraged the public. There was the instance of the fearless fifteen-year-old boy Sushil Sen, who had assaulted a British officer for brutally lathi-charging the crowd in the court. He was dragged off to Kingsford's court and sentenced to fifteen strokes of the lash. With every beating, the boy screamed Bande Mataram, which seemed to reverberate across the country.

The revolutionaries decided that this man had to go. The government was quick to sense that the magistrate's life was in danger, so they transferred him to Muzaffarpur. First a book was sent to him by post. A hole was carved out in the book and a bomb was placed in it, which would explode as soon as the book was opened. Kingsford never opened the book, dispatching it into his cupboard. Then,

46 Sumit Sarkar, 1994. P. 478.

Kshudiram Bose and Prafulla Chaki, young men just out of teens, were sent to the town to do the job. On 30th April 1908, instead of Kingsford, they ended up killing Mrs and Miss Kennedy. On their way back the next day, Kshudiram was arrested. Prafulla took his own life when he was about to be arrested by sub-inspector Nandalal Banerjee at Mokama station in Bihar.

While all this action was keeping the young revolutionaries occupied, Jatin was dealing with the British in his own inimitable way. He was on his way to Darjeeling on an official work tour. The train stopped at Siliguri. There was an ailing passenger in the compartment. She was thirsty, but the water-man was nowhere to be seen. Time was running out and something had to be done immediately. Jatin took a pot and ran to fetch water from the tap. The platform was crowded and approaching the tap was difficult. Moreover, four British officers were marching around, occasionally bullying people. We have already seen that this was nothing unusual in colonial India. The white man thought he was above the law, used filthy expletives to address the locals, and occasionally kicked and punched them. Hurrying to fetch water, Jatin had a minor collision with an officer. Jatin promptly apologized, but the officer picked up his cane and began bashing him. He didn't know that the person he was dealing with was no ordinary man. Jatin didn't say anything at that moment. He calmly filled the pot with water, went back to the compartment and handed it over to the sick person.

When that was done, he went back and landed a punch on that officer's face. The officer fell flat on the platform, his face bleeding. Another officer whipped his lash, while someone else came charging at Jatin with his rifle. Jatin floored them too and the fourth was also dealt with in a similar fashion.

This was a most uncommon scene. People were accustomed to be intimidated by the colonisers, but here was a Bengali youth, paying them back in their own coin. A large crowd gathered and cheered Jatin. Police at the station arrested him, but knowing that he was a government employee going on an assignment, he was released on bail. The incident became sensational news and was widely covered in the press.

When the case came up for hearing in the court, the soldiers were ashamed. They could not explain how they were so summarily dealt with by a bare-handed Bengali youth.

Senior British officials were enraged by the timidity of their men. "Cowards!" they barked. "Firstly, you are so fainthearted that even being armed you cannot tackle an unarmed man? And you have no shame! You have come to the court to seek redressal!"

The soldiers promptly withdrew their complaint. But the magistrate advised Jatin to behave in future. Jatin gave no such assurance. He candidly said he would do it again to save himself or his countrymen. Jatin's boss Wheeler was amused as well as amazed at his physical prowess. He heartily congratulated Jatin.

After the Kennedys were killed in Muzaffarpur, apart from Kshudiram, some others were also arrested on suspicion. They faced terrible torture and intense interrogation in custody and the police came to know about the activities at the country house in Manicktala. Next day, on hearing the news, Aurobindo instructed his brother to remove all incendiary materials like arms, inflammatory literature, etc., from all their hideouts.

Evidently, the boys were too tired and only dug up some holes to hide some of the material. Next day, the police arrived at dawn and rounded up the entire gang. They unearthed some trunks hidden underground, in which they found bombs, dynamite, a revolver and revolutionary literature. Not only that, the police raided other hideouts in the city and also in places like Medinipur, Srirampur, Khulna, Malda and Jessore. They arrested almost everyone from everywhere. The police action was so sweeping and exhaustive that there was literally nobody left to light the lamp in the secret societies.[47]

Jatin was transferred back to Calcutta in June, 1908. It was a terrible time to be in the city. Severe repression had been let loose by the administration. Prevention of Seditious Meetings Act, 1907 and the Explosives Substance Act were strictly enforced. The government came down heavily on meetings and demonstrations, laying down heavy penalty for possessing bomb-making materials.

Anushilan Samiti was banned and so were similar organizations in the district. The Press Act of 1908 was

47 Hem Chandra Kanungo, 2016. P. 164.

enforced, imposing strict censorship. At the same time, the Vernacular Press Act of 1878 was revived. As a result, Bhupendranath was arrested in 1907, purportedly because he was the editor of *Jugantar*. The paper was forced to shut down in 1908.

Brahmabandhav Upadhyay, the editor of *Sandhya* patrika, was arrested on 10th September 1907. He refused to defend himself or take part in the trial, finally meeting his end in custody due to serious ailments on 27th October. *Bande Mataram* was hauled up for publishing seditious articles. Bipin Chandra was summoned for the same. He refused to appear and was sentenced to six months' imprisonment. The paper ceased publication after its editor Aurobindo himself was arrested.

The ripples of the Kennedy murders were also felt in Maharashtra, where *Kesari* was banned. Lokmanya Tilak was sentenced to six years of prison in Mandalya in Burma (now Myanmar) for supporting the so-called terrorist movement in Bengal and for publishing articles in *Kesari* which the authorities deemed as seditious.

The arrests made after the Kennedy murders came to constitute what is famously known as the Alipore Conspiracy Case. Kshudiram was tried at a different court at Muzaffarpur, where he was arrested, and sentenced to death. The Alipore case was the first noteworthy conspiracy case in the country. The Chapekar brothers had been convicted in a general murder case, so the idea of conspiratorial litigation had not been envisioned by the British then. In total, 37 persons were tried. Hearing started on 11th October 1908 at the bench of Judge Beachcroft and ended on 14th April 1909. Verdict was announced on 6th May 1909. Barin Ghosh and Ullaskar Dutta, the chief architect of the bombs, were sentenced to death. Ten men were exiled for life at the Andaman and Nicobar Islands, aptly termed as Kalapani. Three were exiled for ten years, another three for seven and one sentenced to rigorous imprisonment. The rest, including Aurobindo, were freed. Later, on appeal to High Court, death sentences of Barin and Ullaskar were commuted to lifetime exile. Similarly, the punishment of some others was reduced and eight persons were freed. Hence, in total, twelve persons were penalized and twenty-five acquitted.[48]

The task of the police was made easier with Barin confessing. He made a statement in which he did not mention Aurobindo's name and also left out those who helped the organization financially. He persuaded three of his close accomplices to confess. Naren Goswami, who had turned approver, was sensationally murdered in the jail hospital by Kanailal Dutta and Satyendranath Bosu. It is believed that Naren's death also helped in saving Aurobindo from being convicted.

In such an atmosphere of terror, Jatin had to pick up the broken pieces of the movement and carry it ahead. And he had to do it very discreetly, simultaneously balancing his job at the Secretariat. At this time, there was also an immense shortage of men and money. Jatin went to the suburbs and

48 Tarapada Lahiri, 2005. P. 9.

districts, contacting various splinter groups. He tried to co-ordinate between them and build up a federation which later came to be known as the Jugantar group.

The revolutionaries always led a hard life – there was always a scarcity of clothes, books and other essential commodities and bare necessities. Earlier, some zamindars, businessmen and even distinguished people gave donations willingly. But Naren Goswami, in his confession during the Alipore case, let out many names. As a result, the source of the funds dried up. Nobody wanted to risk their neck in the face of mounting repression.

As a natural course of action, dacoity was the other option. Was it right to resort to dacoity to collect money? This question had been debated in the Anushilan Samiti since its inception. Sometime in 1906-07, a secret meeting of the Samiti was held, presided by P. Mitra. Some said we should leave the common people alone and loot government money only. Others argued they didn't have the strength or capacity to attack government institutions. Aurobindo interfered and said that it was not immoral to resort to dacoity for liberating one's own country. That clinched the argument and dacoity became a common practice for collecting funds.

Jatin also felt that there was no other option. Moreover, he felt that some action had to be started to bring up the morale of fellow activists. There was an air of gloom and people also thought that with the arrest of the Manicktala boys and stalwarts like Aurobindo and Tilak, the movement was practically over.

With activists trying hard to initiate the revolt afresh, several actions were taken. When the Alipore case was in progress, Jatin decided to do away with S.I. Nandalal Banerji who had tried to arrest Prafulla, that had led to their comrade's committing suicide. Nandalal was shot to death on 9th November 1908 in an alley close to his house.

Next in line was Ashutosh Biswas, who was the Public Prosecutor in the Alipore case. He was notorious for trying to mete out most stringent punishment to freedom fighters. In the Alipore case, he was trying his best to consign all the detainees to exile. This man had to go, Jatin decided! He sent his daring disciple Charu Bosu to do the needful. Ashutosh was gunned down within the court premises on 10th February 1909. When Charu was brought for trial, he was so fearless that he said there was no need for it and they could go ahead and hang him.

To compensate for the shortage of funds, several dacoities were also resorted to. Another of Jatin's favourite, Narendranath, led the team which looted government funds at the Changripota (now Subhash Nagar) railway station. Narendranath was caught, but was freed because of lack of evidence. Jatin himself led a dacoity expedition to Raita in Nadia on 29th November 1908. According to reports from the Intelligence Bureau (IB), they exchanged the looted ornaments for cash at B. Sarkar's jewellery shop in Calcutta. The amount thus received was close to two thousand rupees, whick looks like a measly sum today.[49]

---

49 Uma Mukherjee, 2005. P. 178.

Narendranath laid low for some time, and a few months later, his team raided a village named Netra, near Diamond Harbour. Both the Changripota and Netra cases and the murder of police officials were investigated by Deputy Superintendent of Police and intelligence officer, Samsul Alam. He was a very valued officer as he knew the network of the various Samitis like the back of his hand. He was proving to be a thorn for the revolutionaries.

But Samsul Alam was not an easy target. Most of the time, he was heavily guarded. One had to wait for the opportune moment to strike. Jatin and his men began to keep a watch on his movements. But who would do the job? A young man, barely eighteen, named Biren Dutta Gupta had arrived from Dacca. Inspired by various revolutionary literature and valiant deeds of the freedom fighters, he was yearning to prove himself. He approached Jatin. Jatin felt he was too young for such a risky job. But Biren kept on pestering him and finally Jatin relented. But how could Biren do the job? He didn't even know Samsul Alam; he couldn't identify him. So he was provided with an escort who would identify the officer.

It was 24th January 1910. Proceedings were going on at the Calcutta High Court. The arena was filled with people, bristling with activities. Biren entered along with his friend and soon the latter spotted Samsul, pointed him out to Biren and moved away. The haughty police officer was ascending the steps. Biren confronted him, "Are you Samsul Alam?" he asked haughtily.

The experienced officer nodded.

Biren smiled, moved closer to him and fired! Drum! The court premises reverberated with the sound of the shots. It was a swift and flawless operation. The dreaded officer lay dead on the floor. There was chaos everywhere. People were in utter panic and ran helter skelter. Constables ran to get hold of Biren.

"Don't dare to come near," he threatened and fired indiscriminately. The crowd moved away from him, looking at him in awe. Finally his ammunition was exhausted and the brave man surrendered.

Three days later, Jatin was arrested. He was accused of being the main conspirator behind the murder. A few days later, he was acquitted of the charge of abetment of murder and immediately re-arrested for being a member of a gang of dacoits. His name had come up in the police list back on 5th November 1909 when one Lalit Chakrabarty had been arrested in Darjeeling. He turned approver and named Jatin, among many others.

The recent spate of violence had rattled the authorities. Once again, a manhunt was launched and many people were rounded up, including Jatin's uncle Lalit Kumar. The case was further complicated when police was able to extract a confession from Biren. They softened up the boy by telling him that he was being maligned by the leaders for sullying the image of the movement by resorting to anarchist activities. They showed him fake newspapers to prove the same. In a feat of excitement, the inexperienced boy blurted out that he was responsible to none but Jatin da. The police now got a golden chance to implicate Jatin in Samsul's murder.

They tried to hold a trial on 20th February, just one day before Biren's execution. But Jatin's barrister J.N. Roy refused to cross-examine a witness at gun point, without knowing the charge against him, and with no opportunity to interview his client. Biren was executed the next day and the Barrister's wile and legal knowledge saved Jatin.[50] Jatin held no grudge against Biren. He knew the spirited boy had been duped by the cunning police officers.

But there were still the dacoity charges. Forty-six men were implicated under section 121A for waging war against the king. This case came to be known as the Howrah Conspiracy Case. The accused were divided into different groups like Shibpur Dal, Kiddirpur Dal, Chingripota Dal, Haludbari Dal, Jugantar, Chhatra Bhandar, etc. The judges opined that these groups were no doubt involved in various criminal activities. But according to their learned opinion, various groups could not be tried under a single conspiracy as no connection could be established between their activities. As a result, except the six who were involved in the Holudbari dacoity, all the others were acquitted.[51]

The Howrah Conspiracy Case also revealed that the revolutionaries had tried to influence personnel of the 10th Jat Regiment. Jatin had met some of them and inspired them to revolt against the British. Other revolutionaries had visited various barracks in north India with credentials

---

50 Uma Mukherjee, 2005. Pp. 178-179.

51 Nalinikishor Guha, 1954. P. 162.

from the officers of the above regiment. These exposures rattled the British because a revolt in the army could once again shake the foundations of the empire, as it had in 1857. They promptly took harsh measures and several officers were court-martialled, the regiment disbanded.[52]

Jatin too was acquitted and released from jail on 21st February 1911.

52 Prithwindra Mukherjee, 2020. P-61

A MEETING OF TWO GREAT MINDS

Three persons who were greatly instrumental in the formation of the Anushilan Samiti departed from the political scene in the years 1910 and 1911. After having been acquitted of all charges in the Alipore Conspiracy Case, Aurobindo came out of jail and found that the political scenario was rather dismal. Tilak was incarcerated in far-flung Burma. Bipin Chandra Pal, after serving his term at Buxar jail, had left for London. Their absence had created a void in the national leadership.

In the given circumstances, Aurobindo started publishing two weekly magazines – *Dharma* and *Karmayogin*. By their very names, we can understand that these were more religious than political in nature. This was a different man, much chastened and spiritual, and the fiery articles he wrote in *Bande Mataram* disappeared. As political disturbances continued unabated, he closeted himself at Chandannagar, a French colony in the Hooghly district.

The police had failed to implicate him due to lack of evidence, but they were convinced that he was the mastermind behind the activities of Barin and the young brigade. The murder of Samsul Alam and the continuing unrest further fuelled their suspicion.

Amidst increasing surveillance, Aurobindo was able to hoodwink the police and travel to Pondicherry (now Puducherry), a French territory beyond the reach of British law. From there, he often communicated with his disciples in Chandannagar. Sometimes, he gave them political advice. But he never again returned to active politics. Aurobindo was considered the Guruji of the organization. His departure was a blow to the morale of the activists. Jatin was particularly crestfallen as he had been initiated into the cult by him.

But that wasn't all. More bad news was in store. On 23rd September 1910, P. Mitra passed away at a time when his beloved organization was facing unprecedented repression. Some had been executed and many more were exiled or languishing in jails. P. Mitra's contribution in strengthening the organization and spreading it far and wide in the districts is unmatched. He shaped and guided the Dacca branch of the Samiti, under the able leadership of Pulinbehari Das, which withstood severe police onslaught, even when the mother organization in Calcutta was in tatters. His death left a big void, as nobody could match his wisdom and organizational capabilities.

Sister Nivedita was away from India during the crucial period from August 1907 to the mid of 1909. After returning, she didn't live for long and breathed her last in Darjeeling on 13th November 1911. Jatin was heartbroken as it was Nivedita who had guided him in social work and introduced him to revolutionary literature. She had often taken Jatin to Swamiji, whom he admired greatly.

While there was a general sense of gloom, owing to these events, two encouraging events occurred during the same time. Rash Behari Bose, who would go on to become a great revolutionary, came to Chandannagar in early 1911. This marked the beginning of his strengthening collaboration with the freedom fighters in Bengal, which would prove to be crucial in the coming years.

More heartening news came at the fag end of the year. On 12th December 1911, the partition of Bengal was annulled by the Viceroy Lord Hardinge. It sent ripples of joy throughout the country, particularly in Bengal. Many lives were lost, many were incarcerated, many were exiled in the inhuman conditions of Andaman and Nicobar islands. Yet, for eight long years, revolutionaries had continued their relentless struggle against the bifurcation of the state.

Finally, as the colonialists wilted, the stand of the revolutionaries was vindicated. West and East Bengal was reunited, and united Bengal was placed under a governor. Bihar and Orissa formed a different province and Assam was placed under a chief commissioner. But this news of joy came with a rider. The vindictive rulers shifted the capital of the country from Calcutta to Delhi. It was becoming increasingly risky for the imperialists to rule from Calcutta. After all, the city, in spite of much repression, continued to be the hub of revolutionary activities. This marked the beginning of the decline of the city as the most vibrant political and financial centre of the country.

On the professional front, Jatin was dismissed from service after his arrest. He appealed against this order as even after a year-long trial, no evidence had been found against him. But Mr Wheeler, his former boss, who had once admired him greatly, now vehemently opposed his reinstatement in the service.[53] Financially, Jatin was in dire straits.

As his name had come up in the police list, he was no longer eligible for any government job. But his family, now living at Jhinaidaha, was entirely dependent on his earnings. His daughter Ashalata was growing up and she needed to go to school. So Jatin went back home. Days passed in uncertainty. Jatin woke up very early, sat aloof and distraught in the verandah adjoining the rooms.

Binodbala understood his pain. She would come and sit silently by his brother, hold him by his shoulders and encourage him. "Don't worry! Bad times will pass."

Jatin rested his head on Didi's shoulder. A breeze blew across the lagoon spread in front of them. The meadows on its sides were glowing with overnight dew. Sparrows were twittering in the courtyard, searching for grains. The sun was just rising and in that ethereal half-light, Jatin felt a strange calm in the presence of Binodbala. It was as if his mother was again by his side.

Why was he brooding? he thought. Hadn't the Maharaj asked him not to brood? Were there not other jobs besides

---

53 Prithwindra Mukherjee, 2020. P. 66.

government service? Millions of people were earning their livelihood doing some job or the other. Why couldn't he? *Come on, get up*! an affectionate voice chided him in his mind.

Suddenly, he stood up, as if jolted out of a reverie. "I can earn a living as a contractor," he declared in a firm voice. "I think I am capable of doing that."

Binodbala was happy to see his resolve. "That's like the brother I have always known. You have always been a fighter. You have overcome so many problems; together, we have witnessed so many losses. And even in such pain, nothing could hold you down. This problem of earning a living is nothing in comparison."

And so it was decided! Jatin took contracts from the Jessore District Board for building roads and bridges. This work needed a lot of travel and Jatin had the opportunity to go to several districts. He travelled on a bicycle or rode a horse. Like in his job at the secretariat, he proved to be very sincere and efficient as a contractor. Under his supervision, various new roads, culverts and bridges were constructed in the districts. In Jessore, he supervised the works of the earth work of the Sara bridge, light-railway between Jhinaidaha and Jessore, a screw-pipe bridge at Jhinaidaha and also the new munsiff court at Magura.

More than ten years later, Saibal Kumar Gupta was posted as Sub Divisional Officer (SDO) at Jhinaidaha. He found the cottage where Jatin lived and the Cassels' bridge over the river Naba-Ganga, the construction of which he had supervised. The locals told him that the then SDO, Mr Cassels – frustrated with the delay of the construction due to the procrastinations of several contractors – had finally got hold of Jatin to finish the job. He had completed the project before the Governor's visit and saved Mr Cassels from embarrassment.[54]

Despite getting appreciated for his work as a contractor, the liberation of the country was never far from his mind. Under the guise of business, he continued organizing secret groups in various districts. Apart from the Anushilan Samiti, most of the splinter groups in various districts came under his influence. The loose federation, which he had formed earlier, which had come to be known as *Jugantar*, was revived again. Young men like Narendranath, Jadugopal, Amarendranath Chatterjee, Nalini Kanta Kar and Bipin Ganguly became his protégés and life-long admirers.

Amarendranath had set up the Sramajibi Samabaya, a general store which was a façade for secret society activities. Hari Kumar Chakrabarty, another close associate of Jatin, set up Harry & Co. in Calcutta. At Baleswar in Orissa, Shaileswar Bose set up Universal Emporium, a cycle and watch shop. All these shops were also fronts for secret society activities, and we find that these will become very important as our narrative progresses.

Jatin used to frequent Sramajibi Samabaya, thus getting acquainted with many activists. In this way, he was able to form a formidable group that considered him as their *Dada*. The people he employed in his work were mostly found to be members of various societies. The police were cunning enough and they never believed that he had retired to an

54 Prithwindra Mukherjee, 2020. P. 67.

apolitical domestic life. They always trailed him. But these police spies, or *tiktikis* as they were popularly known, could not keep up with the speed and dynamism with which Jatin moved around. They were sometimes caught red-handed, which led to hilarious incidents.

During this time, Jatin came across a book named *Germany and the Next War* written by Friedrich Von Bernhardi. In this book, the Germans had tried to gauge the situation in India. They had tried to understand if the rebels in the country could be utilized if there was a war with the British. The author believed that if a war broke out, then the nationalist agitation in India could unite with Pan-Islamism, which could cause a headache for the British. Jatin was very inspired by this book and this triggered his plans to cause an insurrection in the country with the help of foreign powers.

He utilized his contacts to meet with the Crown Prince of Germany (son of Kaiser Wilhelm II) during his visit to Calcutta in 1912. The Prince is said to have given him an assurance that arms and ammunition would be supplied to the Indian revolutionaries.[55] In this way, Jatin made the first noteworthy attempt to seek the help of foreign powers to liberate the country.

This marked a departure from the politics of individual assassinations and dacoities. He had always tried to chart a different path, his own path of social work, guerilla warfare and insurrections. Though, he had to resort to killings and dacoities often, but his big plan was to start an insurrection

55 Prithwindra Mukherjee, 2020. P. 66.

with foreign help and by causing disaffection within the army.

Since the beginning of the twentieth century, sporadic efforts were being made by Indians living abroad to augment the efforts of the revolutionaries in the country by mobilizing men, arms and foreign help. Shyamaji Krishna Verma who founded the Indian House in 1905, which was a shelter for radical Indian students residing abroad. He also ran an English paper, *The Indian Sociologist,* which stridently opposed British rule in India. There was also Madam Bhikaji Cama, who raised the flag of Indian independence at the International Socialist Conference in Stuttgart, Germany in 1907. The flag had the crescent moon and the sun representing Islam and Hinduism. *Bande Mataram* was scripted on the flag.

But the most dynamic and mercurial of all Indian revolutionaries living abroad was Lala Hardayal. He was involved with a secret society in Lahore. But sensing that police were closing in on him, Lala Lajpat Rai[56] persuaded him to leave for Europe in 1908. He dabbled in all kinds of activities and felt attracted to Anarchism, Marxism as well as Buddhism. He gave up studying for ICS and instead became the editor of *Bande Mataram* in Paris. In 1911, he relocated to the west coast of USA. He started organizing the Indians there, particularly the Punjabis. He was one of the founder members of the weekly paper, *The Ghadar* (Ghadar

56 Another Congress leader, the third of the great triumvirate Lal-Bal-Pal (Lala Lajpat Rai, Bal Gangadhar Tilak, Bipin Chandra Pal).

meaning revolt). The masthead of the paper read, *'Angrezi Raj ka Dushman'*, meaning the enemy of the British Raj.

Ghadar was a strictly secular paper which denounced the British Raj in the strongest terms. In one article, the paper pointed out that the British looted 50 crore rupees from India each year; another article stated that they had spent 29.50 crores for the British Indian army, whereas for health, merely 2 crores were assigned. For education, a measly 7.75 crores was spent.

Famine had become recurrent, and in the last decade, two crore people had lost their lives due to hunger. With Indian money and soldiers, the British had attacked Afganistan, Burma, China, Egypt and Persia.

Around this *Ghadar* paper, an organization was also launched. Hardayal aggressively recruited Sikhs and Indians of various nationalities, and trained them. Both, the paper and the party, proudly proclaimed that their religion was patriotism, not Sikhism or any other. Thus, time and again, we find that in spite of the heavy influence of Hindu doctrines and dogma, a subtle but stable flow of religion-free nationalism was always in existence in the Indian politics, both in the country and abroad.

Hardayal and Rash Behari came to know each other through J.M. Chatterjee, a revolutionary who was incidentally in touch with both of them. When Chatterjee himself left for England sensing his imminent arrest, he introduced all his contacts in Lahore and Delhi to Rash Behari. which is why, Hardayal considered Rash Behari as his own man. The latter was then stationed at Dehradun, working for the Forest Research Institute. His residence became the rendezvous for revolutionaries from various places in north India. He had come to Chandannagar hearing of his mother's illness. She died after a few months and Rash Behari stayed on in Chandannagar for a long time. During this time, he came in contact with members of a local society and Anushilan Samiti. This society, named Prabartak Sangha was led by Moti Lal Roy, who was also a close associate of Aurobindo. Thus, the revolutionaries from Bengal and north India came into contact with each other and the Samiti also spread its activities in other parts of the country. This is significant because the Anushilan Samiti later developed into the Hindustan Republican Army (HRA) and then blossomed into Hindustan Socialist Republican Army (HSRA), inspired by the ideals of the legendary Bhagat Singh, Chandrasekhar Azad, Ashfaqullah Khan and Batukeswar Dutta, among others.

A year after the partition of Bengal was annulled, Hardayal in USA was elated and declared to his followers that his man in India had done a great job! What was it that Hardayal was so happy about?

Actually what had happened was that Rash Behari and his accomplices in Chandannagar had hit upon the idea of assassinating Lord Hardinge on the occasion of the announcement of the transfer of capital from Calcutta to Delhi. One day, the members of the group were huddled in a meeting in a room in which Aurobindo used to stay before he moved to Pondicherry. The atmosphere was grim.

"They have shifted the capital from Calcutta! How do we avenge this?" Someone asked.

There was an eerie silence. Summer had set in and the weather was muggy. A fan whirred noisily, making the silence more palpable.

"Let's bomb Hardinge," Shrish Chandra Ghosh, a protégé of Moti Lal, whispered.

Rash Behari immediately sprang to his feet. "This is a great idea," he exclaimed.

"But there will be heavy security. After all, he is the Borolat, Viceroy," someone cautioned.

"We have to plan meticulously, that's all!" Rash Behari brushed aside the apprehensions.

They immediately got into action. Rash Behari selected a young man named Basanta Biswas from his ancestral village Porgacha in Nadia district. He trained Basanta for several months in Dehradun and then took him to Lahore and got him employed there. On 21st December 1912, Basanta moved to Delhi and stayed at the house of a comrade named Amir Chand. On the 23rd, the fateful day, Rash Behari himself arrived in Delhi to personally lead the action. Hereafter, there are several versions of the incident.

The Viceroy sat on a splendidly decorated elephant and the ceremonial procession headed by him was passing through old Delhi. He had his wife by his side. Basanta, who was sitting in an enclosure disguised as a woman, threw the bomb. It instantly killed a servant and the Viceroy himself was seriously injured by the splinters of the bomb.

His wife was unhurt. Both Rash Behari and Basanta melted into the crowd.

The repercussions were massive. There was a brutal lathi-charge on the crowd around. Nobody knows how many died or were injured. The government went mad. That such a daring attack could be carried out in the heart of the new capital unnerved the government.

Hardayal and his friends rejoiced in USA. In India, a huge manhunt was launched to apprehend the culprits. Basanta, Amir Chand and others were arrested and four of them were sentenced to death. The investigations into the incident came to be known as the Delhi Conspiracy Case. Rash Behari managed to evade the dragnet and remained in the shadows. Such was his audacity that he even passed a resolution at the Forest Institute in Dehradun expressing condolence for the attack on the Viceroy.

He had many close shaves with danger. Numerous times, he was able to avoid encounters with the police by sheer common sense. On a certain occasion, he was said to be carried out of his home as a dead body under the very nose of the ever-vigilant police. There were other occasions when he took on the masquerade of a woman and slipped through heavy police cordon placed around his residence. No wonder he is considered a master at hoodwinking the police.

But who actually threw the bomb remained a mystery! It is said that at the last minute, Basanta threw off his women's clothes, came down from a rooftop to the street and threw the bomb. He said the same to Amarendranath while returning to his village at Porgacha. But two years before his death, Rash Behari himself said that he had charged the bomb. His close accomplices too have gone on record affirming the same. According to police records, a man who had been sentenced to the gallows confessed that he had thrown the bomb at Hardinge. His name was not disclosed, but descriptions about the man resemble Basanta. In any case, that the mastermind behind the entire operation was Rash Behari has been proved beyond doubt.

In 1913, there was a major flood in Burdwan and Midnapore districts. Activists of various societies became involved in relief work. Their zeal for social work endeared them to the people and opened up new avenues to spread their revolutionary ideology. In the process of humanitarian work, members of different societies came to know each other. This intimacy led to more cohesiveness between the various groups.

With this development, though, the intelligence department was not amused. They sensed that these men were not merely doing social work, but utilizing this opportunity to spread disaffection among the peasants. Still, they could do nothing but watch with concern.

During this relief work, Jatin came to know Jadugopal Mukherjee and also renewed his contacts with other activists. Amarendranath was also very involved with relief work. It was he who introduced Jatin to Rash Behari. They met at the famous Dakshineswar temple. It turned out to be a historic meeting. Both men were overwhelmed by each other's zeal and commitment to the motherland. They planned an uprising by indoctrinating Indian soldiers. Rash Behari informed that he was trying to infiltrate the military base in Fort William. "Can you take charge of Bengal?" he asked.

Jatin immediately agreed. "Let's try a big revolt, like the one in 1857," he suggested.

Thereafter, they met several times at the premises of the mandir. Rash Behari told Jatin that he was in close contact with a secret society in Benares (now Varanasi) where Sachindra Nath Sanyal had built up a strong base. Thus, he was in control of an impressive network spread in Punjab and United Provinces. Jatin advised Rash Behari to nurture his contacts at Fort William. They discussed all the nitty gritty of starting a nationwide insurrection. They talked about acquisition of money and arms. This meeting led to a series of further meetings in Bengal and later in Benares.

In March 1914, Jatin, Amarendranath and other revolutionaries attended the Ramakrishna Math anniversary. Charles Tegart, Deputy Commissioner of Calcutta Police, a dreaded police officer of the time, noted that Amarendra received financial help from the Mission for flood relief. He, along with Jatin and others, were found catering to the poor and helping the authorities of the Mission to attend to the visitors. He also noted that three members of the Alipore bomb case were also involved in relief activities. It just goes to show that even the activities of a socio-religious organization like the Mission were under the police scanner.[57]

57 Prithwindra Mukherjee, 2020. P. 69.

By the middle of 1914, war had become imminent in Europe. On 4th August 1914, Germany invaded Belgium, and within a few days, the German army was ranged against the triple entente of Britain, France and Russia. The tension and excitement of war rippled across to Calcutta. *Britain was engaged in a deadly struggle; this is the time to strike,* everyone thought. The secret societies became active. They were urgently in need of arms. Bombs had become scarce ever since the workshop at Manicktala was exposed and closed down. Now there was only one important bomb-making workshop at Chandannagar. There was heavy shortage of firearms as well. Generally revolvers were bought second-hand from ex-armymen, sailors, Anglo-Indians or forcibly seized from security personnel. Jatin bought revolvers from one Nur Khan of Chetla in south Calcutta, through Charu Ghosh, who lived in the same area.[58]

But this was hardly enough. It was then that the daring plan of looting arms of M/S Rodda & Co. came up. It was one of the biggest dealers of arms in the city. This company kept Mauser pistols, manufactured in Germany and considered very powerful. When fitted with their wooden cases, these Mausers became as good as rifles. Atmonnati Samiti and Mukti Sangha of Dacca, which were then maintaining a low profile, led this action. Srish Mitra of Atmonnati was the pivotal point around whom the entire operation was planned. He was the Sircar or the man in-charge for the Customs office of Rodda & Co. He got the information that

58 Uma Mukherjee, 2005. P. 65.

a large consignment of Mauser pistols had arrived from Europe, which needed to be taken to the company's godown.

On receiving the news, Srish and other revolutionaries held a secret meeting on the night of 24th August at Chatawala Gali. The operation was planned and work allotted to different groups. One group was assigned to keep watch on the intelligence officials posted at Dalhousie Square, Calcutta's central business area. Another group was stationed nearby, that could watch out for any danger and immediately caution by singing. The meeting ended and the leaders of the group dispersed. There was a slight drizzle, but hardly any wind. It felt hot and suffocating. No wonder people were out of their homes and loitering on the streets. Amidst them, they hurried through the lanes, careful not to raise any suspicion. They met again at Bowbazar in the house of Srish Mitra. Srish laid out the plan.

"Anukul, you will arrange a cart. The bullock must be strong and sturdy," he instructed Anukul Mukherjee. Anukul nodded.

"And you Haridas, you will have to masquerade as a Hindustani *garwan*.[59]

Everybody laughed.

"For that, he will have to get a fauji-like haircut," someone joked.

"Yes, that he will have to!" Srish agreed.

On the fateful day, 26th August 1914, at about 9 a.m., the group met at Malanga Lane, near Bowbazar. Everyone was amazed as Haridas looked exactly like a garwan. His

59 Cart-driver.

hair was short and spiked, under which his skull glistened. He wore an unclean dhoti hitched up to his thighs, and a shabby sleeveless vest. A brass locket tied around his neck by a black thread hung over the vest. Anukul had arranged a cart and he assured everyone that the bullocks were strong. Srish gave three loaded revolvers to Haridas and two other revolutionaries, Khagen Das and Srish Pal.

"You two will walk by his side, and if you are detected, you will fire," Srish Mitra instructed Khagen and Srish Pal.

"There is a crowbar kept in the cart," Srish Mitra then turned to Haridas. "If firing begins, then you break open a box with that crowbar, bring out a Mauser and get into action." By then, everyone had learnt how to use the modern gun.

Three hours later, at around noon, Haridas arrived at Dalhousie with his cart. It was a cloudy day and the sun was benign. But due to high humidity, it felt uncomfortable. Two men appeared, their waists bulging, and walked by his side.

"Why are you so late!" Srish Mitra shouted at the garwan. Like a true Babu, he glared at the hapless Hindustani.

"Come, let's hurry up!" he barked, exhorting the cart-driver to get on with it.

He then escorted Haridas' cart along with six other carts to the customs house. There Haridas' cart was packed with maximum pistols and ammunition. "Hurry up! Hurry up!" Srish Mitra kept on whispering.

Haridas, like an expert garwan, followed six other carts to the office of the Rodda company. Khagen and Srish Pal almost ran alongside him. All three were perspiring heavily. Srish Mitra was at the head of all the carts, shouting out orders. It was office time and the roads were crowded. The carts meandered through the traffic. Suddenly, a herd of bullocks appeared out of nowhere. The animals moved leisurely through the vehicles. Everything came to a standstill. Horns blared, drivers shouted. Nothing moved, except the burly animals. A posse of policemen came running. Haridas cast a furtive glance at others. Their faces had turned pale. Their hands were on their hips.

"*Jaldi karo, jaldi*!" A policeman slapped the behind of the herdsman. Another landed his baton on the back of a buffalo. Minutes passed and Haridas could hear his own heartbeats. A whistle blew and the vehicles began to move again. They almost ran. Somewhere along the way, Haridas took the by-lanes of Dalhousie, managed to outwit the police, the intelligence, and arrived at a godown which belonged to a friend of Atmonnati. Here, Anukul took delivery of the goods. Srish Mitra delivered the six carts at the company's office, arrived in a huff, and joined his friends at that godown.

"I must leave," he announced dramatically.

Along with Srish Pal, he left Calcutta that evening itself by Darjeeling mail. Strangely, no trace of him has been found ever again. According to the police, the seventh cart having ten packages of arms was missing and Babu Srish Mitra absconded from that day. It is assumed that he died or was killed in an attempt to escape from India.

These arms were distributed to various destinations in Calcutta and even outside the province. This pistol became a very valuable weapon for the revolutionaries. Rash Behari carried a Mauser, and Jatin and his friends fought their last battle with the police at Baleshwar using these pistols. The other incidents in which these arms were used were Garden Reach, Gazipura, Haripur, Beliaghata, Shibpur, Salkia, etc. Unfortunately, some of the arms and ammunition were later recovered as well.[60]

Around this period, there was a lot of excitement among the revolutionaries abroad. The war had opened up new opportunities to strike at the British government. High officials in Germany talked of a war-time collaboration between the Germans and the Indian revolutionaries. These officials felt that creating an upsurge in India would help them to win the war.

During September 1914, Virendranath Chattopadhyaya and Dr Abinash Chandra Bhattacharya met Baron Max von Oppenheim, the German foreign minister, and obtained an assurance of supply of money and arms to augment an uprising in India. They formed a committee to work out this plan. It came to be known as Indian Independence Committee, which later became the popular Berlin Committee. It immediately began to reach out to Indians living abroad.

The Committee had an expansive plan. It wanted to capture the Andaman islands and set free the revolutionaries imprisoned there. They would join an expeditionary force of Indians and Germans who would attack India through Siam (now Thailand) and Burma. Three German war ships

60 Uma Mukherjee, 2005. Pp. 65-75.

with German officers and men would bolster this force. One of the ships would come to the Bengal coast and the other proceed to western coast. Most importantly, the Committee decided to send arms to India by the sea. Later, Jatin was informed of this by Jitendra Nath Lahiri in March 1915 and he banked on this support to begin an insurrection in the country.

Years after, it was found that the German government had a comprehensive plan of fuelling rebellion through three fronts. They nurtured a scheme through the north-western part of India, known as the Afghan scheme. This scheme resulted in the formation of a provisional government of India in Kabul on 1st December 1915. Raja Mahendra Pratap was President; Maulana Barkatullah Bhopali, the Prime Minister; and Maulana Abaidullah Sindhi, the Home Minister. Due to lack of support from the Afghan government, this scheme collapsed.

The other two schemes of the German government are known as the Bangkok scheme and the Batavia (now Jakarta) scheme. The latter was a plan to fuel a rebellion in Bengal and was linked with Jatin and his group's grand vision to start an insurrection in Bengal, which would later spread to the rest of the country.

The Bangkok scheme, on the other hand, depended on the Ghadar revolutionaries who were coming back to India in large numbers, specifically to start an uprising. This scheme was mainly related to the vision of Rash Behari to start a revolt in north India and Punjab, for which he had given the responsibility of Bengal to Jatin. For the success of this scheme, the arrival of the Ghadar revolutionaries was crucial.

The Ghadar party abroad was making huge preparations for what they thought would be a final showdown with the government. On 31st December 1913, they held a big meeting at Sacramento in USA. There, they showed photos and news reels on India's great revolutionaries, and explosive slogans were raised against the British. Hardayal gave a fiery speech in which he exhorted everybody to go to India, as Germany was to soon declare war against Britain. Hardayal travelled to various places and continued to give such bold speeches. It attracted the attention of the US government and the maverick leader was arrested on 16th March 1914. He was declared an 'unwanted foreigner', released on bail and asked to leave the country. Hardayal took shelter in Switzerland. His arrest and deportation further enraged the Sikhs and other Indians in US and Canada. At this time, a revolutionary pamphlet was circulated in which there was a poem where eminent freedom fighters like Tilak, Aurobindo, Haradayal, Barkatullah urged all Indians to go back to their motherland and join in the struggle to liberate their motherland.

Ghadar Patrika gave a clarion call – For organizing this revolution in India, we need courageous soldiers; their salary is death; their prize is the honour that is bestowed on a martyr; their old age emolument is freedom; the battlefield is Bharatbarsha. The Patrika laid out the tasks after returning to India – distribute Ghadar literature; uproot the railway lines; withdraw all your money from banks; encourage Indian soldiers to revolt.[61] This charged up the masses and many people decided to go back to India.

The call of Ghadar reached the Indians who lived in south-east Asia. They mainly worked as coolies and low-wage workers and their lives were miserable. They had always been deliberating on migrating to Canada where they expected to get a better pay. A contractor named Gurdit Singh led these people. He hired a ship named Komagata Maru, which literally means a transport ship. This ship transported coal. He converted it into a passenger ship and picked up Sikhs from Hong Kong, Shanghai, Yokohama and other places and sailed for Vancouver on 4th April 1914. It was not merely revolutionary fervour which inspired Gurdit to take this step. He wanted to ensure that his compatriots get a better living and he wanted to protest against Canada's 'Foreign Nationals Entry Act' which he thought was tyrannical. According to this act, you had to deposit two hundred dollars to enter the country and you had to be coming directly from your own country, not some other country. Moreover, they behaved very harshly with Indians. Canada's Sikhs were already agitating against this draconian act and Gurdit wanted to strengthen that agitation.

On 23rd May, the ship reached Vancouver port. After reaching, the Sikhs became more volatile. Their brethren in the town supplied them with arms, so that they could fight with the local police. Canada government did not allow

61 Suprakash Roy, 1949. Pp. 260-267.

the passengers to land as they did not have the required deposit money, and also since they were not coming directly from India. This further enraged the Sikhs, both in the town and on the ship. Ghadar party continued their relentless propaganda to revolt against the authorities. Canada government got scared and asked the ship to leave the port. When they refused, a huge contingent of police was sent. But they were repelled by continuous fire from the rebels. The police fled. The desperate government now took the unprecedented step of sending war-ships against a passenger ship. It was an unequal battle. Komagata Maru finally left the port.

In the entire episode, the role of the British government was dubious. They made no effort to help the passengers on the ship; nor did they try to convince the Canada government to allow the Sikhs to enter that country. Instead, they asked the Canada government to send the ship back to India. The passengers wanted to go back to where they had come from, but the permission was denied. They wanted to alight at Hong Kong and Singapore, but they were denied on the pretext of the war. The British wanted to pack them off to Punjab and teach them a lesson.

Finally, on 29th September 1914, Komagata Maru docked at the Budge Budge port on the river Hugli near Calcutta. A special train was kept ready to herd the passengers off to Punjab. The Sikhs refused to board the train. An army platoon was kept at hand for such an eventuality. They obstructed the Sikhs and the latter retaliated. A gun fight that resulted from it, led to many dead and injured.

According to government estimates, eighteen Sikhs had died; there were casualties on the other side also, but it was not acknowledged. Gurdit Singh fled along with a large contingent. Many were taken prisoners. Rest were forced into the train and sent to Punjab.[62]

The news of the massacre spread like wild fire. Punjab was seething. Many Sikhs returned to Punjab from across the world. Among them were a few Ghadar leaders as well. The ground was fertile for a revolt. It only needed a spark.

62 Suprakash Roy, 1949. P. 267.

A REVOLUTION THAT NEVER WAS

Rash Behari had been living stealthily, in hiding, since the abortive attempt on Viceroy Hardinge's life. Some days after that incident, he went to Chandannagar and remained in hiding. He lived in a locked room, going out for his ablutions after darkness. Even then, he could not avoid the watchful Calcutta police.

On 8th March, his house was raided by the police led by Godfrey Denham, a top-level intelligence officer, and Tegart. They laid a siege on his house, but failed to trace him. They were befuddled. Rash Behari, as has been already stated, was a master at hoodwinking the police. The officers later confessed in a confidential report that they were unable to find the great leader, even when he lurked nearby. He fooled them by watching the entire police raid from behind a mango tree.[63]

Later, he moved to Benares and continued working in secret. A reward had been declared for his arrest, his photographs were published everywhere, yet he continued

63 Uma Mukherjee, 2005. P. 134.

to escape the police dragnet. In Benares, he repeatedly changed his residence and was always able to stay a step ahead of the intelligence officials. Even under such pressure, he began to organize the movement in United Provinces, Punjab and Bengal.

In November 1914, he came in contact with a young firebrand, named Vishnu Ganesh Pingley. He was a Marathi from Telegaon Dhamdhere in Puna. He was a member of the Ghadar party and lived in the US. He returned to India and came to know Satyen Sen, a close accomplice of Jatin. Satyen had also returned from abroad to inform Jatin that the Germans were ready to help with money and arms. This was the news Jatin and his group had been waiting for. Satyen introduced Pingley to Jatin. He held many discussions with the young man and then sent him to Rash Behari. This was around November 1914.

Jatin also went to Benares along with Narendranath and some others to visit Rash Behari, to put the final touches to their planning. They had different approaches regarding the revolt they wanted to initiate. It has been earlier mentioned that after the Alipore Bomb case and the ban on secret societies, Jatin had brought various splinter groups together, which came to be known as the Jugantar Party. The Anushilan Samiti, though banned, kept itself afloat under various disguises. Most importantly, it maintained its own identity and did not merge with Jugantar. There was no animosity between the two groups. In fact, they often co-operated with each other. But regarding help from Germany, they had different views.

Rash Behari looked up to Jatin as an elder brother. When they met in Benares, he spoke frankly with him. He had reservations about getting arms from Germany. Not that he was aversive to foreign help, but he thought the plan was fraught with too many uncertainties.

"Look, it looks improbable to me. Hope you understand," Rash Behari told Jatin respectfully. The latter smiled and nudged him to elaborate.

"It's doubtful if the arms will reach India at all. And even if they reach, you have to unload and store, then you have to distribute to various places, some quite far-flung. How can this entire operation be done in secret? As it is, the police is always after us…" Rash Behari trailed off.

Jatin's face was impassive, but he listened to his younger colleague intently.

"Then there is the matter of training the activists in using these sophisticated arms. But if you really can overcome all these hurdles, we will help you in every possible way; that's our commitment," Rash Behari said in a rush, as if relieved that he had been able to provide some assurance to his elder brother.

"Yes, there are risks," Jatin agreed. Then he fell silent. "But how can you keep silent? The enemy must fear you. If you don't strike, they will not fear."

Looking at Rash Behari confidently, he said, "Don't worry. We have everything arranged. Rest is…" He looked up towards the ceiling, suggesting it would finally boil down to god's will and destiny. "We will get in touch with you as soon as we make some progress," Jatin said in a firm voice.

"Our planning is…" Rash Behari hesitated in sharing his plan of action.

"Please go ahead. I am willing to help," Jatin assured him.

That put Rash Behari at ease. He finally overcame his hesitation and told Jatin, "We are trying to trigger a soldiers' rebellion. Our men are already trying to influence the Indian soldiers. They have a lot of resentment, as they are treated shabbily, humiliatingly. They are waiting for a chance to strike back." Rash Behari's eyes glowed.

Jatin was highly impressed and promised to help. "We in Bengal will provide you all the help you require."

Rash Behari was elated. The two leaders fixed the date of the uprising as 21st February 1915.

After Jatin left for Calcutta, Rash Behari immediately got into action. Pingley, one of the most spirited and enthusiastic revolutionaries, informed him that nearly four thousand men had arrived from the US and they were all ready for the rebellion. Rash Behari sent him and Sachindra to Punjab to gauge the situation there. Pingley told the Ghadar men that he had established contacts with Bengal revolutionaries. This motivated the Ghadar men because they were not able to do anything substantial because of a lack of leadership. Pingley arranged a meeting at which looting of treasuries, indoctrination of troops, making of bombs and dacoities were discussed. It was decided that some men will be taught bomb-making under the leadership of Rash Behari.

Rash Behari himself went to Amritsar in January 1915. Bomb-making was started in real earnest, even factories came up at various places in Punjab. Many dacoities were committed to raise funds. The most important part was seducing the Indians in the British army. For this, men were deputed at various towns which had large army cantonments. Contact was established with twenty-six cantonments, including those at Jabalpur, Rawalpindi, Meerut, Ferozepur, Benares, Allahabad, Ambala, among others. Rash Behari moved to Lahore to supervise the preparations. He also tried to organize the villagers so that they would rally in support of the soldiers.

On 12th February, Rash Behari announced the date of the revolt – 21st February. It would be a countrywide uprising spread from Peshawar to Bengal. Tri-coloured flags were made, which would be raised everywhere. The three colours of the flag were yellow, red and blue, representing the Sikhs, Hindus and Muslims, respectively. In Bengal, the Anushilan Samiti kept its activists ready. Uniforms were made for them so they could be identified as revolutionaries. They kept a large stock of bombs. As soon as the revolt began, bombs would be exploded in large numbers in front of important government strongholds. It was decided that the Punjab mail's failure to reach Howrah station in the morning will mean that the uprising had begun. There was a huge suspense. Units of revolutionaries all over the country were literally on tenterhooks. The D-Day had finally arrived!

But nothing happened. The uprising never occurred. One man named Kripal Singh turned traitor. He had managed to become a member of the core group of revolutionaries. His movements had already raised suspicions and Rash Behari had been notified about the same. He sent orders to finish him off. Sensing the collapse of the plan, the astute leader antedated the rising and fixed it for the 19th. But this information was also passed on to the police by Kripal Singh.

Barely eight hours before the revolt was to begin, the police raided several hideouts. Late on the night of 19th February, Rash Behari's house was raided. He, along with Pingley, managed to escape. But eight Ghadar men were arrested and a large cache of bombs, firearms and radical literature was found. Thus, the hub of the revolutionaries was cracked. Simultaneous raids were launched on several cantonments across the country. Hundreds of soldiers were disarmed, hundreds of activists arrested. Punjab in particular was ransacked. A total of nine conspiracy trials took place in Lahore. Twenty-eight persons were sentenced to death, twenty-nine acquitted and the rest were sentenced to transportation and imprisonment.

Undeterred by the failure, Pingley still tried to seduce the soldiers of the Meerut cantonment. But again, he was fooled by a person posing as a revolutionary. He was caught red-handed with a box of ten highly powerful bombs. He was sentenced to death. Later, Viceroy Hardinge intervened and commuted the death sentence of seventeen men to transportation for life. Pingley and the rest were told that their death sentence would also be reduced if they pleaded for mercy. But the brave revolutionary along with ten others preferred to go to the gallows.[64]

Rash Behari remained at Benares for about a month, eluding the police that pursued him relentlessly. After putting the Benares unit in order, he shifted to Chandannagar. The failure of the rising greatly disturbed him. He now became convinced that without foreign assistance, it was impossible to liberate the country. He decided to leave for Japan. It was decided that he would travel in the name of P.N. Tagore, posing as a relative of Rabindranath Tagore, who was scheduled to visit Japan shortly. It was as if he was preceding the poet to make arrangements for his stay in that country. On 12th May 1915, the leader, somewhat disillusioned, left the country in a steamship named Sanuti Maru. He arrived in Japan on 5th June and soon began to work for India's liberation with renewed vigour.[65]

On 15th February, a mutiny of Indian soldiers, predominantly Muslim, was suppressed brutally in the island-state Singapore. The 5th Light Infantry Regiment was ready to embark on a voyage to Hong Kong, ostensibly to proceed to the war raging in Europe. The Regiment had eight companies, out of which, four consisting of Muslim Rajput soldiers, with a few Jats and Lohias, revolted. They seized control of the city for almost a week. This has come to be known as the Singapore mutiny, the details of which are shrouded in mystery even to this day.

64 Buddhadev Bhattacharya, 1979. Pp. 108-109.

65 Uma Mukherjee, 2005. P. 146.

At least one thousand soldiers ran amok, killing twelve British officers and fourteen Europeans. They liberated German prisoners, some of whom joined the mutineers. Many theories have been put forward to locate the reasons for the revolt. One is that, it was a conspiracy hatched by the Ghadar party. Though the Ghadarites took credit for it, no evidence of their involvement has ever been found. Second, it was thought to be a German conspiracy and supposedly a rumour had been spread that the German king had converted to Islam, and that it was not right to fight against a fellow religionist. Third was the reluctance of the rebels to fight against Turkey, under the Caliph of Islam. The most logical reason seems to be the miserable conditions under which the Indian soldiers had to work. They were bullied and humiliated by the British officials. The British put it in a different way, saying that there was a lack of leadership and sacked the CO of the regiment. Over and above, the soldiers were reluctant to proceed to the terrible war that had unfolded in Europe.

By 22nd February, the revolt had been crushed with the help of combined forces from France, Russia and Japan. Forty-seven soldiers of various ranks were court-martialled. Two of the supposed ring leaders – Subedar Dunde Khan, Jemadar Chisti Khan – were the first to be shot on 21st February. Sixty-four were transported for life. No memorial or plaque honouring these brave men exists anywhere. Western accounts continue to vilify them and yet they are found nowhere in Indian history. No attempt has yet been made to accord them their deserved place in the annals of Indian freedom movement. In fact, they are not even recognized as freedom fighters.[66]

The news of the Singapore revolt barely reached Calcutta. But the departure of Rash Behari left a big void in the movement. Nevertheless, there was no time to brood. Even as the preparations for the countrywide uprising were going on, Jatin had insisted upon raising one lakh rupees in a week. Accordingly, plans were hatched to commit a number of dacoities. The first target was the South India jute mills at Garden Reach, an area adjacent to Calcutta.

On 12th February, a Babu, along with two *durwans*, boarded a horse-driven cart from the company's head office. They had Rs 18,000 with them for payment of wages and bonus to the workers. The revolutionaries led by Narendranath took a taxi from Howrah and reached Garden Reach crossing around 3 p.m. As the horse-cart arrived, they obstructed it by parking the taxi across the road. They forced the people out and got hold of the cash-box. Passersby were awestruck seeing such a heist in broad daylight. But they didn't dare come close as the group was armed. The driver of the taxi panicked and refused to co-operate. He was severely thrashed and thrown out of the vehicle. One member of the group sat at the wheel and they drove to Baruipur, a small town about thirty kilometres from the city. But further trouble awaited them. The tire of the taxi burst. Thereafter, they changed several vehicles,

---

66 https://m.timesofindia.com/india/singapore-mutiny-of-1915-a-standalone-episode........updated. Accessed on 3rd August 2014.

travelled through different places and finally arrived in Calcutta. Two of them were later arrested and imprisoned for several years. Even Narendranath was arrested, which upset Jatin, as he was the closest comrade. In desperation, he even planned to hijack him from the police van when he would be taken to court. However, it was not required and Narendranath was freed on bail.

Another dacoity was committed ten days later. This time, the target was a rich businessman in Beliaghata. He was supposedly robbed of Rs 32,000 and here also, the group came in a taxi. The driver again refused to drive and had to be killed. Unfortunately, when the cash box was opened a few days later, it was found to be filled with papers rather than currency notes. To make up for the failure of the Beliaghata dacoity, another attempt was made at Pragpur in Nadia district. This attempt too failed and resulted in the tragic death of Sushil Sen, the fearless boy who had developed into a fiery revolutionary.

A very serious shortcoming of the movement has to be noted here. These recurring incidents show that the common people had no knowledge of the activities of the revolutionaries. That is why drivers of vehicles refused to co-operate. The masses mostly remained aloof, or were awe-struck. In some instances, they even opposed the freedom fighters. It shows that there was barely any attempt to involve the people, or to convince them that the revolutionaries were fighting to liberate the country. There was hardly any effort to do sustained work among the students, peasants and other sections of the society. This continued to be a severe weakness of the revolutionary movement ever since its inception and would prove to be very costly in future.

In early March 1915, Jitendra Nath Lahiri of the Berlin Committee arrived in India with the news that arms would be sent by the sea. The revolutionaries in Bengal were asked to send someone to Batavia to guide the Germans for the shipment of arms to Indian shores. A meeting was called, which was attended by Jatin, Amarendranath, Bipin Ganguly and others. Everyone insisted that Jatin should leave India as he had become a marked man. But Jatin steadfastly refused to go and said he preferred to die in the country rather than go abroad. Narendranath was not present in the meeting. Jatin proposed his name to go to Batavia and everyone agreed. Jatin took the responsibility of arranging the funds for regular contact with the German consulates in Bangkok, Batavia and Shanghai.

The recent spate of dacoities along with the murder of S.I. Suresh Mukherjee on 28th February became a grave concern for the government. Even when various bids to cause uprising proved to be abortive, even when renowned leaders had departed from the scene for some reason or other, even when hundreds had been martyred, incarcerated, exiled, the efforts to destabilize the Raj continued relentlessly.

The Rowlatt report of 1918 notes that 1915 was a remarkable year for a number of outrages. It said that using taxis for robbery was a new method of revolutionary crime introduced by Jatin Mukherjee and his group. It was a method invented by Jules Joseph Bonnet (1876-1912) in France. This method had struck terror in the police ranks and the government introduced armoured cars, flying squads, drop-gates on avenues, check-posts, sirens in the police stations and armed sentries posted at important junctions of the city. People and vehicles were subjected to random searches. Rewards were announced for apprehending Jatin, dead or alive.[67]

It was becoming increasingly risky for Jatin to remain in Calcutta or its vicinity. One day, Jatin was in a secret meeting when he suddenly saw a flickering shadow near the door.

"Jatin da, are you there?" Someone called out.

Jatin da! Who is this man? Jatin was alarmed. He jumped up from his seat. *How did he recognize him? How did he know that he was there?*

"Shoot him! Kill!" Jatin screamed.

Chittapriya, who was with him, leapt out of the room. "Who are you?" He threatened.

"Nirad, Nirad Halder. Is Dada there?" came the answer.

Chittapriya fired. Droom! Droom! Everyone fled from that hideout. Nirad was mortally injured, but he didn't die. In his dying declaration, he named Jatin as the assassin.

This proved to be the last straw. Everyone felt it was time for their leader to go underground. But where could he go!

---

67 Prithwindra Mukherjee, 2020. P. 79.

"I think Baleshwar will be safe," Nalini said rather uncertainly, suggesting a coastal town of Orissa (now Odisha), nearly 250 km from Calcutta.

Narendranath looked at Nalini. "Are you sure?"

Nalini kept quiet.

"We can go and check," Narendranath suggested.

But again, Jatin refused to move unless others like Bipin Ganguli, Chittapriya were given similar protection. When he was assured that all the absconders along with him will be moved to a safe place, he relented. And so the duo proceeded to that place to check the facilities at Nalini's place.

They went beyond Baleshwar to Mayurbhanj, then a princely state, thirty-five miles away. Here they found a suitable place at Kaptipada with the help of Manindra Nath Chakrabarty. Manindra's father Kedar Nath Chakrabarty was a police inspector and also the Diwan of Kaptipada. Kedar Nath was gifted the village Mahuldiha by the Raja of Kaptipada. This property was inherited by Manindra. After the assassination of Samsul Alam, Nalini had fled from Calcutta and took shelter in this village. He started a business which was, in fact, a front for secret society activities. They were satisfied with the arrangement and the information was passed on to Kolkata. Nalini had already built a cottage there. Together, they started improving the facilities so that Dada and his men could stay comfortably.

Some days before proceeding to Baleshwar, one evening, Jatin became emotional. He bared his heart to his friends.

"Bengali youth has become ineffectual due to living a sheltered life for ages," he shook his head disapprovingly.

Then looking at the expectant faces, his voice rose, "Now I want to push them into battle with guns blazing." Jadugopal, who was among the audience, felt a shiver pass through his body.

"This much we will have to do," he continued, his eyes glowing. "We will have to prove that the Bengali youth can strike back." His voice electrified everybody.

"Even a coward could become courageous in his presence," Jadugopal was to reminiscence years later.

Binodbala had written to his brother in a letter, "It is fine that you have responded to the call of the country. But let it never be said that the lion has been caged."

They will not have me alive, this promise he had made to himself. "The mother whose milk nourished me will ensure that I will do something worthwhile before I leave."

There was another important point Jadugopal had discussed with his Dada. "The government is denigrating us as anarchists, dacoits. We will have to counter this. Let us make soldiers' uniforms, so that people can identify us as revolutionaries." Jatin had agreed to both the points. However, tragically, these could not be implemented in time.[68]

In early April, Jatin, along with his closest colleagues, went to the Ganga ghat and hired a boat. It was still spring, the month of Chaitra, but the sun was already radiant and sharp. They arrived at the station and took a train to Bagnan, a big village, fifty-five kilometres from the city.

---

68 Jadugopal Mukhopadhya, 1982. P. 363-364.

Jadugopal writes in *Biplobi Jiboner Smriti* that before the train left, Ramchandra Majumdar told others, "We are handing over the heart of Bengal to you. I am not exaggerating a bit. Mind your responsibilities." Everyone sat spellbound, determination writ large on their faces.

Jatin spent some days at the house of Atul Sen, Headmaster of the local high school and a member of Jugantar group. From here, they moved to Tamluk and then to Kumar-ara, a village near Mahishadal in Medinipur district. Here they stayed at the house of Hemchandra Mukherjee, principal pundit at Bagnan High School. They were now closer to their final destination, which was about 140 kilometres away. By now, photos of Jatin had been circulated widely, monetary reward for apprehending him had also been increased.

After the preparations were complete, Narendranath came back. He and Jatin boarded a train from Panskura, which would take them to Baleshwar. Other men had boarded the same train from Howrah. In the train, they came across two rowdy Anglo-Indians. They insisted that Jatin and Narendranath vacate their seats. They used foul language, and gesticulated wildly. Everyone was armed, but even without arms, Jatin alone could have floored the two boors and thrown them out of the train. But he remained remarkably calm and vacated his seat. Obviously, he didn't want to create a ruckus which would attract the police.

At Kaptipada, Jatin became Ramanand Swami, a tall and dignified sadhu attired in ochre robes. His four comrades-in-arms were Chittapriya Ray Chaudhuri, Niren

Dasgupta, Manoranjan Sengupta and Jyotishchandra Pal. They took on the pseudonyms Kalidas Ray, Shambhu Ray, Jogananda Ray, and Prabodh Ray, respectively. Here, a brief introduction of these four valiant young men who were with Jatin in the final battle would not be out of place. Needless to say, all four were astute followers of their Dada. They could go to any length to protect him.

Chittapriya was the son of an affluent landlord. His family was Tantrik and he himself was very spiritual. Niren's father was an Ayurvedic doctor. He was a dare-devil man, prone to take high risks. Manoranjan and Niren both were from Madaripur, now in Bangladesh. They were intimate friends. Manoranjan's father was an accountant in a local estate. He was a very jolly person, always bubbling with energy. Jyotish was the son of a potter. Among the four, he was the only one married, who also had a little daughter. He and Nalini Kar had helped Jatin in his contractor business.

The house where they stayed had several rooms. There was a large courtyard in which was a tree which had bullet marks; obviously it was used for target practice. There was also a wrestling pit. The residents regularly practiced shooting and wrestling.[69]

Narendranath went back to Calcutta and sailed for Batavia from Madras in April, 1915. He took on the pseudonym C.A. Martin and became a pucca sahib. He wore European dress, spoke chaste English with proper accent.

---

69 Prithwindra Mukherjee, 2020. Pp. 89-90.

Mr Griffiths of Madras National Bank later gave a vivid description of him to Denham. "Appeared to be almost certainly a Bengali; age about 23-25 years; height about 5′6″ to 5′7″; fairly well-built and having a slim and wiry appearance; thin face and hair cut in European fashion; noticeably dark complexion; clean-shaven; good-looking; sharp features; talked English very well and appeared to be thoroughly bright and intelligent person; wore European clothes similar to those in India in the hot weather."[70]

After reaching Batavia, he contacted the German Consul who informed him that a ship named Maverick with a cargo of arms and ammunition had left California and was on its way to Karachi to help the Indian revolutionaries. Narendranath requested the Consul to send it to Bengal instead of Karachi. The Consul agreed and it was decided that the ship will anchor at Raimangal, in the Sunderbans. He immediately sent a wire to Harry & Sons in Calcutta, stating that business was promising. This ship was supposed to carry thirty thousand rifles with four hundred cartridges for each and two lakh rupees.

Narendranath then came in contact with Atmaram, a Ghadar revolutionary active in Java, Siam, Batavia. He helped to get money from the Germans, which would be sent to various addresses in Calcutta in instalments. These places were Sramajibi Samabaya and Harry & Sons, about which we have briefly discussed earlier. The former

---

70 Uma Mukherjee, 2005. P. 198.

was set up by Amarendranath and the latter by Hari Kumar Chakrabarty, who belonged to the same village as Narendranath. Hari Kumar had also set up a cycle shop named Universal Emporium at Baleshwar under the charge of Shaileswar Bose. All these shops served as fronts for secret society activities.

All in all, four transactions took place between Siam, Batavia and Calcutta. On 29th June, five thousand rupees were sent to Eastern Bank, Calcutta to be paid to Harry & Sons. Accordingly, Hari Kumar collected the payment from the bank on 3rd July. The second transaction occurred on 13th July when Hongkong and Shanghai Bank received a sum of ten thousand rupees to be paid to Harry & Sons. This telegraphic transfer was encashed by Hari Kumar in three instalments, through a new account he had opened at the Co-operative Hindustan Bank. So in June and July, a total of fifteen thousand rupees was transferred to the revolutionaries in Calcutta. Needless to say, all communications regarding these two transactions were carried out in coded language.

After ensuring the delivery of arms and money, Narendranath decided to return to India to supervise the delivery of arms. He set sail from Batavia on S.S.Golconda and arrived at Negapatam on 14th June. Next day, he took a train to Madras. He had with him a draft of eighteen thousand rupees, payable to C.A. Martin or bearer. He presented the draft to the Madras National Bank, but

Mr. Griffiths, an official of the bank, refused to pay him and asked him to wait for the next day. He talked with Narendranath for about half an hour and later gave a graphic description of him to Denham, which has been reproduced earlier.

Perhaps sensing danger, Narendranath refused to stay at Madras. That very evening, he wired Jadugopal that he had returned and was starting for Baleshwar. He transferred the draft to Amarendranath, who presented it for collection in his full signature and address at National Bank, Calcutta. It was sent for collection and was finally paid to him on 7th July. These three transactions consecutively and other suspicious circumstances like the disappearance of Jatin and his friends finally alerted the intelligence officials. Before the fourth transaction could materialize, there was a police raid on Harry & Sons on 7th August. Hari Kumar and two others were arrested. A remittance of Rs 9670 from Batavia was intercepted by the police. [71]

Jatin and his followers were meanwhile having a joyous time at Kaptipada. There was no fear of the police here, no constant surveillance, and no tiktiki following you everywhere. The pressure off, everybody was in a good mood.

Jatin had turned his abode into an ashram. He had a *rudraksh* bead tied to his neck and he looked like a real saint. He became known as Swamiji and people flocked to meet him, to pay their obeisance, and to seek his advice to overcome their problems. He practiced homeopathy

71 Uma Mukherjee, 2005. Pp. 195-201.

and knew the use of Tincture iodine and quinine. He even brought helpless villagers to his place and treated them. They used to pay *dakshina,* gift to the Brahmin, all of which was utilized for revolutionary work.

Summer was harsh that year and large parts of Orissa were ravaged by drought. Close on the heels of the drought came famine, and then the inevitable epidemic. To fight the calamity, Jatin and his followers began tilling the land. They began to grow cereals, which were distributed freely to the villagers. But that proved too little for so many people. One rare day, all of them decided to have a good meal. Chittapriya cooked goat's meat and everybody was getting ready to partake of the sumptuous lunch. Suddenly, out of nowhere, a group of tribals arrived and asked for rice. Jatin invited them to sit and eat to their heart's content. His followers were dumbstruck; they were looking forward to this meal. But like their leader, they showed no disappointment and fed the tribals. Yet, food was so scarce that people ate barks of trees, creepers, grass and leaves. Dysentery was rampant, and cholera broke out. They tried their best to serve the people, but Chittapriya himself fell sick and Jatin nursed him day and night.[72]

On 16th March 1915, a ship named Annie Larsen, with a cargo of arms and ammunition left the Californian port of San Diego and arrived at Soccorro Island near Mexico. Another ship Maverick, sailed from San Pedro, near Los Angeles on 23rd April. It would receive the arms from Annie Larsen and transport it to India. Annie Larsen waited at the

72 Prithwindra Mukherjee, 2020. P. 198.

islands off Mexico for three weeks, waiting for Maverick to arrive. Then it ran short of fresh water and provisions and wandered off to a port near Washington, where it was seized by the US officials. When Maverick at last reached Soccorro Islands, it learnt that Annie Larsen had left thirteen days ago. It waited vainly for about a month, hoping to receive its cargo of arms and ammunition. It too wandered around moving from port to port, raising suspicion all around, finally reaching Java on 15th July. A few days later, it was seized by Dutch warships.[73]

It is believed that a Czech named Emanuel Victor Voska had leaked the plan to the Allied Forces. In USA, Czech and Indian patriots were friends. Both were trying to shake off foreign rule, hence the intimacy. The Czechs got a hint of the armed conspiracy. They were against the Austria-Hungary block and supported the Allies, the British-French-Russian entente. They passed off the information to the French, who informed the British and the plan was doomed.[74] If this man Emanuel Voska had not informed Tomas Masaryk, who happened to become the first President of Czech Republic in 1918, India would have attained independence much before than it actually did. Masaryk has himself mentioned these facts in his memoirs, *The Making of a State: Memoirs and Observations, 1914-1918*.

---

73 Uma Mukherjee, 2005. Pp. 201-204.

74 Jadugopal Mukhopadhyay, 1982. P-330

A REVOLUTIONERY DIES, THE NATION RISES

Narendranath arrived at Baleshwar from Madras and met Shaileswar Bose at the Universal Emporium. From there, he proceeded to Kaptipada to meet his beloved Dada. He had brought a sackful of gold *mohurs* which he poured in front of Jatin. Jadugopal and others also came down from Calcutta. The supply of arms having been confirmed, they began the planning for the insurrection. It was decided that the uprising would begin in the villages where tri-coloured flags (green, white and yellow) would be hoisted.

Close to one thousand khaki uniforms were made ready and distributed at various centres in Calcutta. There was an important military base located at the Chandipur coast near Baleshwar. This would be the next target of attack. Attempts would be made to involve the tribals and spread the revolt into Medinipur and Birbhum districts. The bridge on the river Ajay would be blown off. Jatin himself took on the responsibility of cutting off the Madras railway while Bhola Nath Chatterjee was given the responsibility to deal with the Bengal-Nagpur railway. Dynamites were stocked to blow off the bridges. Telegraph lines would be cut off. When all the incoming railway routes were blocked, communications disrupted, Fort William would be attacked. Arms and arsenal would be seized and the enemy soldiers disarmed. For this, work had begun to indoctrinate some soldiers at the Fort William.

After receiving the arms at Raimangal, it would be distributed to three places. One lot would be sent to Hatia (located in Noakhali district in Bangladesh) to take control of the eastern districts. Here, an uprising would be organized with the help of the members of Dacca Anushilan Samiti. Another consignment would be sent to Narendranath and Bipin Ganguly in Calcutta to attack Fort William. The third consignment was to be sent to Jatin to spread the uprising in Orissa.

Accordingly, a group of activists led by Jadugopal arrived at Raimangal to take the delivery of the arms. Earlier a team had come to arrange the equipments required for unloading the arms. It was the rainy season, and dark clouds hovered in the sky; gusty wind blew and there was a frequent drizzle. Jadugopal and his men waited for ten days in this stormy weather, straining their eyes for a glimpse of the lights of an approaching ship which was supposed to arrive on 1st July. But those lights were never seen. The Maverick didn't arrive. By the middle of the month, a man named Kumud Mukherjee, who was travelling to Java from Calcutta, came across a newspaper report in Singapore which stated that the Maverick had reached Java empty. He passed on the news along with the paper cutting to Jadugopal in Calcutta.

The revolutionaries were devastated. Another attempt at an uprising had failed.

Jadugopal himself delivered the news to Jatin at Kaptipada. It shocked everybody. They had expected challenges like delay, but not such a turn out in the wildest of their dreams. They had pinned so many hopes on the faith that the arms would arrive. Everyone's face fell. There was pin drop silence. But Jatin was calm, aloof.

"God has rectified our decision," his steady voice broke the silence. "We wanted to free the country with help from foreign powers. But India must rise from within, with her own strength."

Narendranath was disappointed, but he wanted to have another try. He was determined to visit Batavia again and talk to the Germans. "I will not return without arms," he pledged.

Jatin looked at him affectionately and said softly, "Come back soon, with or without arms." Later, Narendranath – after having metamorphosed into M.N. Roy – was to write in his memoirs that Dada's words were an order for me. "He was not only our Dada, but our Commander-in-Chief."[75] Accordingly, he again sailed on 15th August.

To make matters worse, the raid at Harry & Sons in Calcutta on 7th August gave the police the clue to the existence of the Universal Emporium in Balasore. Denham, Tegart and Leslie Newman Bird (Deputy Commissioner of Police) promptly moved to Baleshwar. They contacted District Magistrate Kilby and asked him to mobilize a

75 Prithwindra Mukherjee, 2020. P. 100.

strong force. On 5th September, they raided the Universal Emporium and arrested Shaileswar Bose and two others. Here, they found the name of Kaptipada written on a piece of paper. Overnight, they mobilized the security forces of Baleshwar and the princely states of Nilgiri and Mayurbhanj. They reached Kaptipada and stayed at the local dak-bungalow. They rode on elephants. The bail of the elephants alerted the villagers, who informed Jatin. He immediately asked everyone to get ready. Chittapriya and Manoranjan were then with him, but Niren and Jyotish were living at Taldihi, at a distance of twelve miles. They began to walk towards that place, followed by their faithful domestic help. Manindra advised Jatin to proceed towards the hills and flee. But Jatin would have none of it; he was determined to face the situation.

On the morning of 7th September 1915, the police party was joined by the DIG of Bihar, Railyand. They went to the house they had intel about, but found no one there. They ransacked the house and found some books, the Singapore paper cutting, and an exercise book in which Jatin had expressed his thoughts. Manindra told the police that they had come for contractor business, and had left. The police party left for Baleshwar after keeping some guards posted there. Around 11 o'clock in the night, someone called out "Dada, Dada," at Manindra's window. It was Jatin. He asked for fifty rupees and a pistol. Manindra again requested him to flee by the hillside.

Jatin was enraged. "How long will we continue hiding like this, just for the sake of saving our lives? We will let them know who we are!"

Manindra was dumbstruck. He was amazed by the determination of the man. He bowed his head in admiration; he dare not restrain him.

On 8th September, Jatin and others went to Baleshwar station and boarded a train. The train was almost empty, with practically no passengers. They suspected that these few passengers must be police informers. They got down and tore their tickets and started walking towards the villages. Meanwhile, the cunning British had spread the rumour that German and Bengali dacoits were on the run. They announced a reward of two hundred rupees for each of them. It created a stir among the villagers; the promised amount was a lot of money for these impoverished people.

Suddenly, villagers started following them. They brandished arms and shouted 'dacoits', 'dacoits'! Jatin remembered they had decided to make uniforms to avoid such ugly situations; situations in which your own people turned against you. But alas, it could not be implemented. It was drizzling, the ground was slushy. Everyone was tired, famished. They occasionally sat and lay down to rest. But they laboured on! For almost two days, they had been on the road in that inclement weather, with villagers hard on their heels.

On 9th September morning, they reached the village Gobindapur near the river Buribalam. It was the month of Bhadra and the river was brimming over. No boats were available. They saw a boat carrying wood. After a lot of persuasion, the *majhi*[76] agreed to take them across. When he saw the group walking towards the jungle, he became suspicious. He informed the local Dafadar. He was not at home, but his brother, along with a few men, tried to chase the group. They fired in the air and the villagers retreated. But the relief was short-lived. Soon, a large crowd led by the village headman Raj Mohanty blocked their passage. The fugitives tried hard to convince them that they were not dacoits, but to no avail. Someone fired and Mohanty died on the spot. Others fled; some went to Baleshwar to inform the police.

They arrived at a village named Damuda. Here, they stopped at a small shop and quickly ate whatever was available. When they started their journey again, the villagers were again on their trail. No amount of request, persuasion or threat could stop them. The lure of easy money was too much for the villagers to overcome. The revolutionaries felt helpless.

Manoranjan fired, and again, there were some casualties. Half a mile away, there was a small stream near Chaskhand. Balancing their weapons and clothes on their heads, they swam across the river. They took position behind a high ant-hill. It was a tall mound, a vantage point with clear view on both the sides. Unknown to them, another man draped in torn shabby clothes also crossed the stream. He took position on the top of a tree. He was a sub-inspector named Chintamoni Sahu.

---

76 Literally, boatman.

Around two o'clock, the message reached the police that the fugitives had been sighted. A large force led by Kilby, Railyand and Staff Sergeant William Rutherford hurried to the spot. When they were searching for the exact spot where Jatin and his followers had taken position, they spotted Sahu frantically signalling them with a cloth from atop a tree. They immediately started firing with long-range rifles. When they found there was no retaliatory fire from the other side, they began creeping nearer to the mound. Jatin allowed the police to come closer. By not firing back, he had led them to believe that the revolutionaries had no long-range arms. When they were close enough, there was a burst of constant fire from behind the mound. The attackers scampered for cover. Some lay prostrate behind the ridges of the paddy field. Some panicked and ran backwards to find safer spots. It was never known how many of them died or were injured; the colonialists did not want to give the rebels the credit of having hurt the imperial forces.

It was an unequal battle. Yet, due to the sheer grit and determination of Jatin and his men, the battle went on for almost two hours. A five-man ragtag army held out against a formidable British force. But they were succumbing gradually. Their strength was ebbing, their ammunition was fast depleting. They had a small leather bag in which there were ample cartridges. Unfortunately, the key to that bag was lost. Unable to vanquish the brave enemy with conventional tactics, a subedar went up on a tree to have a better view. Chittapriya had just then raised his head to fire. He became an easy target and was promptly shot on the head. He collapsed in a heap. His beloved Dada held him in his arms. Jatin's left palm was injured too, and he was firing with the other hand. Just then, bullets pierced his stomach and jaw. Jyotish too was hit and writhing in pain. Jatin knew that the inevitable end had arrived. He knew he would not survive. The end was near, he was certain. But he also knew that he may have been defeated in this physical fight, but his spirit could not be destroyed. Just as his Didi had cautioned, 'The lion would not be caged.'

Not wanting to risk the lives of his comrades any further, he asked them to raise the white cloth. Someone ran to a puddle and brought water to feed the valiant men gasping for breath. There are several other accounts that deny any mention of a surrender. But one common thing that all of them mention is that Niren and Manoranjan were tending to the injured when they were surrounded and captured.

The sun was then setting on the banks of the Buri Balam river. It was also setting on the first important frontal battle with the British since 1857. That night, Jatin was admitted in the emergency ward of the Baleshwar hospital. Writhing in pain on the bed, he declared, "Remember, I alone am responsible for all that was done. They were mere boys, all innocent. Please see that they are acquitted.[77]

Jatin had shared his last thoughts with Dr Satyendra Nath Gangopadhyay.

"Now it's my turn, doctor. The auspicious moment for us to sacrifice our lives has arrived. The firing began again… hail of bullets coming from everywhere, front and back, left and

---

77 Prithwindra Mukherjee, 2020. P. 116.

right. The distance between us and them was decreasing… the bridge between life and death was collapsing. Then I lost consciousness. Don't know when I awoke again. Jyotish was lying injured beside me. Manoranjan and Niren had raised their hands to surrender… Know what, doctor! Our freedom will surely come. The shackle of bondage will be torn..."[78]

***

Jatin breathed his last on 10th September 1915.

The British paid no heed to his request. Niren and Manoranjan were detained in a police lock-up and later sentenced to death. Chittapriya had already breathed his last at the battlefield. Jyotish was transported for life. He later turned insane and died in the Berhampore Jail in 1924.

Niren's and Manoranjan's death sentence was executed on 3rd December 1915 at the Baleshwar jail. The day before their death sentence, both wrote to Bhupati Majumdar, a close friend of Jatin and his group.

"Dada, tomorrow is the Bijaya Dashami of our life. Finally we will take leave of you and our beloved motherland… before we leave, we will continue to pray for the liberation of our motherland. If this promise remains unfulfilled, we pray we may again be born here to fulfill our unfinished task."[79]

---

78 Jadugopal Mukhopadhyay, 1982. P. 340-348

79 Ibid. P. 349.

EPILOGUE

Bhupendra Kumar Dutta, a freedom fighter, who is famous for his 78 days-long hunger strike in Bilaspur jail, has reminisced how a pall of gloom spread over the country after the death of Jatin and the other revolutionaries came to be known. He tried to convince everyone that a revolution could not die with the demise of its leader. In 1923, he mooted the proposal for celebrating Jatin Mukherjee's death anniversary. His intimate circle, including Amarendranath, responded enthusiastically. The latter consulted with Deshbandhu Chittaranjan Das.

It was decided that a delegation would visit Baleshwar and arrange to erect a memorial in the name of the martyrs. The word spread and Bhagat Singh, the legendary revolutionary, requested Bhupendra to send Jatin and other martyrs' photos and information on the battle. Thus the eighth anniversary of Jatin and his friends' death was celebrated across the country from Baleshwar to Bengal and Benares to Punjab. On that day, a daily named *Swadesh* was released which was replete with the photos and exploits of the heroes.[80]

---

80 Prithwindra Mukherjee, 2020. P. 129.

This celebration and many other acts of daring and defiance underlined the fact that the battle of Buri Balam may have been lost, but the war against the British imperialists continued unabated. The trend of seeking foreign help to liberate the country did not end with the glorious martyrdom of Jatin and his comrades.

Even after the failure of the Maverick episode, German officials continued their efforts to supply arms to the revolutionaries in Bengal. They were aided in their efforts by Rash Behari Bose from Japan and Narendranath from Batavia. According to the Sedition Committee Report after the Maverick failed, the German Consul-General at Shanghai arranged to send two other ships to the Bay of Bengal – one to Raimangal and the other to Balasore.

The first ship was to carry rifles, pistols, cartridges, grenades, explosives and a sum of two lah rupees. The other one was loaded with various firearms and explosives as well. A third ship with a massive cargo of arms was to proceed to the Andamans and raid Port Blair. The soldiers in the ship would free the convicts and ransack the dreaded harbour town before proceeding to Rangoon.

Years later, in 1943, Rash Behari reminiscing his younger days wrote, "With the aid of Germany, I was to send home two ship-loads of arms and ammunition, but unfortunately, they were confiscated before reaching India."

Narendranath, on the other hand, pointed out to the Germans that Raimangal was no longer a safe landing-place, and that it was better to send the arms to Hatia. He also wrote in his memoirs that the plan was "to storm the

Andaman islands and free and arm the prisoners there, and land the army of liberation on the Orissa coast."[81]

Needless to say, these efforts did not materialize. After USA joined the war in 1917, it became increasingly difficult for revolutionaries to work from there, and with the defeat of Germany, foreign help gradually dried up. After a lull of few years, Rash Behari formed the Indian Independence League (IIL) in Japan in 1924. The military might of Japan was then soaring at such a pace that it terrified the traditional powers like Britain and France.

In the 1930s, war clouds again began to gather over Europe and renewed efforts to seek foreign help began to crystallize. The activities of the IIL inevitably led to the formation of the Indian National Army (INA). Rash Behari played a pivotal role in shaping the INA and then handed over its reins to the legendary Subhas Chandra Bose, also known as Netaji.

Jatindranath Mukherjee was one of the pioneers to engage the British in a frontal battle. That baton was taken over by Subhas Bose and so the story of India's liberation continued.

We have seen that frustrated by repeated failures, Narendranath, in an impulse, had again started out for Batavia in search of arms. He was accompanied by Phanindra Nath Chakrabarty alias William Arthur Payne. Narendranath visited his old contacts, but this time, the response of the German officials was rather cold. Even then, he didn't give up and sent Phanindra to Shanghai to meet

---

81 Uma Mukherjee, 2005. P. 224.

the German Consul-General. But Phanindra was arrested and the mission collapsed even before it started.

For about a year, Narendranath shuttled between various centres in Far East Asia, persistently trying to send arms to India. When all his efforts came to naught, he went to San Francisco in June 1916. The *Daily Mail* published in the city remarked on his arrival that a "man of mystery" named Chas. A. Martin had landed in the port from a ship named Nippon Maru which had arrived from Hongkong. The newspaper reported that notwithstanding his name on the documentation, the man "is a Hindu and a high-caste Brahmin". The said Martin purportedly declared that he had boarded the ship from a French-Indian port and that he was proceeding to Paris to study. Passengers, however, refuted whatever he said and believed that he was either a revolutionary or an emissary of the British government.

Narendranath's own version states that after he reached San Francisco, the next morning newspapers carried the banner headline: "Mysterious Alien reaches America: Famous Brahmin Revolutionary or Dangerous German Spy." Reading the reports, he sensed danger and immediately proceeded to a town named Palo Alto where the Stanford University is situated. There he met Dhanagopal Mukherjee, Jadugopal's brother and a student of the university. Dhanagopal advised Narendranath to wipe off his past and begin his life afresh. Accordingly, that very day, Narendranath ceased to exist and M.N. Roy was born.[82]

---

82 Uma Mukherjee, 2005. Pp. 210-211.

Few lives have been as eventful as his. He founded the Communist Party of Mexico in 1919. He was a delegate at the second World Congress of the Communist International. In 1920, he founded the Communist Party of India (Tashkent group). During the Quit India movement, he blatantly supported the British and was disgraced. Thereafter, his standing was severely dented and his popularity waned. In later years, he became an advocate of what he called 'Radical Humanism', which has aroused some interest in recent years.

With the departure of Narendranath, the mantle of leadership of Jatin's group fell on Jadugopal. On the night of the battle at Chaskhand, he, along with two other comrades, had reached Baleshwar. They sensed something amiss, so they had proceeded further south. At Cuttack, he learnt of the tragedy from one Nemai Bose.[83]

Expectedly, the death of Jatin was a huge setback for the movement. Many were arrested or deported to the Andamans. Funds became scarce and young men, who were active in the revolution, were forced to go into hiding. But even amidst these adversities, revolutionary fire was not fully extinguished.

There were efforts to unite what the police intelligence termed the eastern and western factions of the party. A few successful dacoities were carried out and police officials murdered. For a few months, Jadugopal had taken shelter at Chandannagar, the French colony which had turned into a haven for absconders. He was in hiding, but he

83 Jadugopal Mukhopadhyay, 1982. P-562

didn't stop functioning. He sent Bhola Nath Chatterjee and Benoy Bhusan Dutta to Goa, then a Portuguese colony, to communicate with Narendranath. Their code message sent to the latter was intercepted by the British and they were arrested. Both succumbed to police interrogation and admitted their role in the German-aided plot. Bhola Nath, unfortunately, committed suicide while in detention at the Puna jail.

Undeterred, Jadugopal kept on trying to establish contact with foreign sources. He had sent another emissary - Santipada Mukherjee – to the Far East to trace Narendranath. But this attempt also turned out to be abortive. Then he instructed Bhupati Majumder to visit USA to establish contact with the revolutionaries there. But Bhupati was arrested on the Pacific, much before he had even reached the shores of America.

Amidst this unprecedented vigil and police repression, the only consistent activity the revolutionaries were able to carry out was publication of seditious writings, both in English and Bengali. These were of course clandestinely distributed among the public, but few were also sent to eminent persons. One letter was even sent to the American President Woodrow Wilson through a barrister named Subramaniya Aiyar, drawing his attention to the cause of India's independence. It urged the President to help the just cause of India and enable the country to throw off the shackles of imperialism.[84]

---

84 Uma Mukherjee, 2005. Pp. 221-229.

On 21st December 1919, a Royal Proclamation was announced, granting amnesty to persons convicted of sedition and cognate offences. This led to some relaxation in the suffocating terror that had been unleashed by the British. The revolutionaries breathed easy for some time till the next spurt in the freedom movement.

While Jatin's close companions somehow survived, the news of his death sent his family into a perpetual stupor. They didn't believe it. Binodbala didn't believe that his valiant brother, the legendary tiger-slayer, could be killed by the British.

She remembered what she had once written to Jatin: "The one that loves you more than any of us is, Himself, constantly taking care of you. O God, what good can we do you, by worrying, by worrying for you?"

But Jatin had prepared her and Indubala for such a tragic eventuality. Even in the most arduous circumstances, family was never out of his mind. Writing to Binodbala from his hideout at Kaptipada on 18th May 1915, he reminisced about their mother:

> *Everybody can complain and can moan; if you and me, on our turn, we stooped to it, why do we chose to be born in the womb of our mother Sharatshashi… We are not like the others children of a faithless and chicken-hearted mother; never forget all that she endured with a smile, throughout her life. Had she been on earth, today, she would have undoubtedly congratulated me for the activities I have chosen.*

Since she is no more, will not the person to whom my mother confided me, my own sister, who means as much as my mother…want to consider for a while and decide what should be now her duty?… I can decently hope that the strength of your soul is today a good deal more intense. Be kind to quieten your mind and to protect Indu with her children. Do not spare any effort so that the children are reared like human creatures (worthy of this name). In moments of need, call one of the brothers[85]*… They will refuse nothing coming from you.*

It is clear from the letter that four months before his martyrdom, he was clear about the fate that awaited him. He writes to Indubala in a similar vein:

"In ever so many ways did I prepare you for the situation which prevails around us today, warning you that it would certainly occur one day, even asking you to get ready for it… All that I wish from you is to be the person among so many thousands in whom, above all, blossom simultaneously strength, patience and a sense of duty. Do not forget to be attentive so that in the future the children can be identified as a (true) man's offspring…[86]

85 Referring to political associates and his followers.

86 Prithwindra Mukherjee, 2020. PP. 122-123.

Postface

On a hot summer day in the month of May 2022, we travelled in a car through the lanes and by-lanes of a posh locality in south Kolkata. It was almost 11 a.m. and the sun was bright and blazing, creating imaginary waves on the road ahead. We were searching for an address; the address of the house of the family of the great patriot Jatindranath Mukherjee, more famously known as Bagha Jatin.

No shopkeeper or passerby knew his name, but an elderly man gave us the direction after we fished out the exact location – 48, Ballygunge Place. We parked in front of a house which looked pale but robust in spite of its age. All its doors and windows were shut, understandably due to the stifling heat. A plaque fixed on the top of the entrance showed that we had knocked on the correct address.

Jatin's grandson Soumendranath Mukherjee greeted us. He is the eldest son of Jatin's youngest son Birendranath Mukherjee, who was only two years old when his father was killed in action. A tall and well-built man, age had apparently not impaired him in any way.

We entered a small sitting room, the walls of which were adorned with framed black and white photographs. There

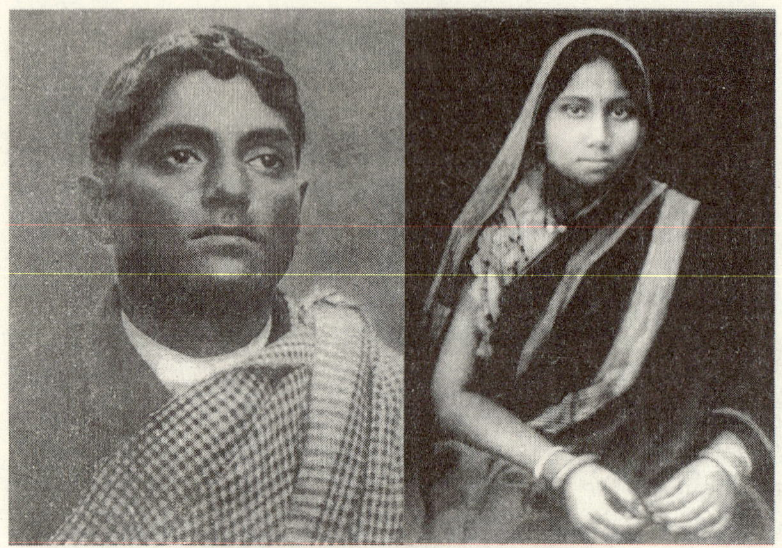

Jatindranath Mukherjee in 1909, from Calcutta State Archive.

Indubala Debi, Jatin Da's wife. Photograph by Supriya Bhattacharjee.

The stamp issued by the government in honour of the revolutionary, from the Calcutta State Archives.

A family portrait from 1912,
from the archives of Dr Prithwindra Mukherjee.
With wife Indubala, his sister Binodbala, and children.

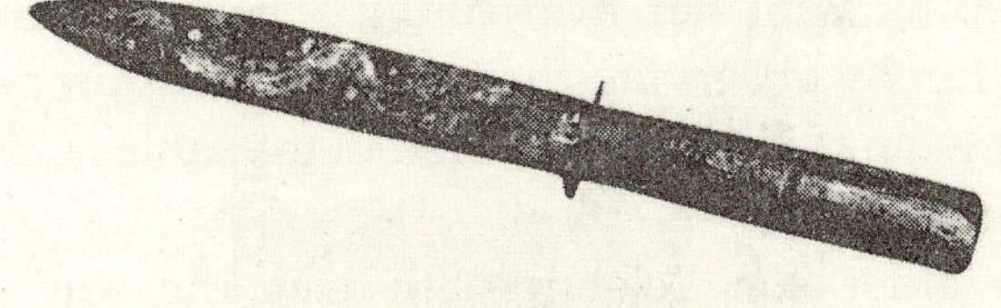

The khukri used by Bagha Jatin
to slay the tiger.
Photograph by Supriya Bhattacharjee.

were small and large photos of Jatin in a familiar pose. He looked young, handsome, well-dressed, hair neatly parted, gazing out of the frame with quiet, expressive eyes. There was also a bust of the man made of plaster of paris, under which is inscribed his famous saying, "We will die; nation will rise."

There was a large photograph of Indubala Debi, the quintessential Bengali housewife, simple yet dignified. There were also photographs of Binodbala, Soumendranath's parents and Bholanath Giri, the Godman.

After Jatin's death, the family shifted to Kolkata and the 'brothers' arranged this house. "Our grandmother died in this house, but she never believed that her husband was dead," said Soumendranath. Jatin's friend Barrister J.N. Roy carried Tegart's message to the family which confirmed that Jatindranath Mukherjee had passed away at Baleshwar. Indubala didn't believe it. She never believed she was a widow. She waited and waited, till she breathed her last in 1937.

In keeping with her firm conviction, family members cremated her by observing the funeral rites appropriate for a married woman.[87] Binodbala died in the same house a few years later.

Jatin's elder son Tejendranath was the sole earning member of the family. Due to some unfortunate family mishap, he left his job and shifted to Pondicherry with his family. Aurobindo Ghosh, who was still alive and had started an *ashram* in the town, came to know about them

87 Prithwindra Mukherjee, 2020. P. 125.

and promptly made arrangements to settle them. After the elder brother's departure, Birendranath's family was in dire straits as he had no source of income. Again, the 'brothers' came forward to help. They contacted Bhupati Majumder, who was then a minister in the Congress government in West Bengal. He told Dr Bidhan Chandra Roy, the chief minister, that Bagha Jatin's son had no means of income. The latter was alarmed and immediately arranged for his employment at the State Transport Corporation.

"Our *pishima* (Jatin's daughter Ashalata), also lived in this house for some years. In fact, *pishemoshai* (Ashalata's husband) died in this house," Soumendranath said.

A biographical film was made on the great man by Hiralal Sen in 1958. A postal stamp was issued in his name in 1970 to mark his contribution to the country. On the occasion of the release of the stamp, Birendranath was felicitated at Mahajati Sadan, Soumendranath reminisced. In 2015, celebrating the centenary of his martyrdom, political leaders hailed his courage and sacrifice. Many offered homage at the memorial at Chaskhand, a few kilometers from Baleshwar. On every death anniversary, some officials or politicians make a beeline to the place to offer their respect. But the memorial itself lies in a decrepit state, calling for urgent repairs and renovation.

"Actually, times have changed," Soumendranath says with a wry smile. "How many people know about the freedom fighters today, forget about emulating them?"

It was well past noon and time to leave. Outside, the sun still glistened, the road and the neighbouring houses sparkled. Our car started and as it rolled, I looked back to see Soumendranath waving. I also had a last glimpse of the house where history sat quiet and anonymous.

APPENDIX-I

JATIN DA

BY MANABENDRANATH ROY (FORMERLY KNOWN AS NARENDRANATH BHATTACHARYA)

We used to call him Dada. In a land and time of Dadas, he was exceptional; there was no one else like him. Like in modern art, during our early days in politics, 'Dadaism' was an unreasonable doctrine. Jatin da didn't care about Dadaism, nor was he a proponent of it. All other Dadas practiced the art of charming others; Jatin Mukherjee was an exception. This quality was inherent in him; he didn't have to practice it. That is why his competitors considered him an enigma, even a depressed person. He didn't have to charm someone to entice someone. He was universally popular to the extent that disciples of other Dadas also liked him.

He was a man of immense physical strength, which made him a legend. Yet his appearance didn't reflect that. Besides, he was an expert wrestler, but he never bragged about his qualities. In later life, I came in touch with many great men, men of immense quality and distinction. But Jatin da was a good man, an honest man. I haven't seen anyone more honest. He was the model, the ideal man. These type of men do not leave their footprints on time. Self-seclusion is their natural calling. It is these men who uphold the beacon of hope piercing the darkness that enshroud the common men. A good man rarely finds his place among great men. This trend will continue till righteousness or magnanimity is considered as a hallmark of greatness.

Jatin da was not a mediaeval knight; he wasn't a person of any particular era. He believed in humanism which transcended the boundaries of nation and time. He believed himself to be a Karmayogi, and that is the spirit he instilled in us. A real Karmayogi is one who does not envelope himself in needless secrecy.... Jatin da was a genuine humanist, perhaps the first in modern India.[88]

M.N. Roy also fondly writes: "The time has changed; the man who earned fame as a great conspirator against the imperialist state and an extraordinarily bold revolutionary is now to be memorialized as a great man in the history of modern India. His birthday is celebrated, and biographies written. But since his time, the political stage of India has been crowded with people claiming niches in history, if not places of honour in the pantheon of the great. Judged by his actual feats, minus the legends woven around them, Jatinda's name may be crowded out of the national heroes...."[89]

---

88 Mani Bagchi, 1968.

89 Source: millenniumpost.in/opinion---'Forgotten Martyrdom' by Rup Narayan Das on 8th September 2021.

APPENDIX-II

AN ANALYSIS OF THE BALASORE BATTLE BY JADUGOPAL MUKHOPADHYAY

At a press conference held on 8th September 1947 at 116, Vivekananda Road, Calcutta, Dr Jadugopal Mukhopadhyay explained the background of the battle of Balasore led by Jatin Mukherjee. He said, "It's wrong to say that the revolutionaries were mere terrorists and they had no idealism. We wanted to create a Republic of Indian Federation on the basis of social, economic and political realities." He said Jatin Mukherjee was the acknowledged leader of the revolutionaries of Bengal.

From the beginning, the revolutionaries began working with a specific plan. Analysing the 1857 revolt, they had found that lack of popular support was the root cause of its failure. Accordingly, they had started working among the students, workers, peasants and the armed forces. Dr Mukhopadhyay said that his party led both the coachmen strike of October 1905 and the strike of the tram workers in

1907...They had also sent men to England to train them to work among the armed forces.

Dr Mukhopadhyay opined that the First World War stimulated their revolutionary activities, but they had thought the war will commence four years later. They had planned accordingly. But the war started in 1914. Then they had tried to bring various groups together and Jatin Mukherjee led this effort. Except the Dacca Anushilan Samiti, all groups came together.

The veteran leader also dwelt on their relationship with the Germans and said that they had received some financial assistance from them, but arms and ammunition didn't reach them. Two ships from Germany stacked with armaments were apprehended in the Pacific Ocean. Due to betrayal, they were deprived of German assistance... Reflecting on their efforts during wartime, he said they had wanted to establish a provisional government. In 1915, such a government had been established in Afganistan, led by Raja Mahendra Pratap. Their attempt was to trigger an armed revolt in the armed forces and also among the civilians. Railway lines and bridges would be destroyed and they would install people's rule in the countryside. They had banked on receiving arms from Germany, which would be distributed to every corner in the country. But the capture of those two ships belied all their hopes. There were then close to fourteen thousand British soldiers in India. They had sent their plan to Germany and the latter had also approved it.

Jatin Mukherjee had gone to Baleshwar to arrange for the distribution of the arms that would arrive from Germany and also to arrange for hideouts for the absconders.

Asked about the flag of their party, Dr Mukhopadhyay said it would be square. Its top, middle and the lower portion would be red, white and green, respectively. They had planned to raise the flag at the Fort William. *'Janani Jonmobhumishco Sworgadopi Goriyosi'* would be inscribed in the middle of the flag. (Loosely translated, it means 'Mother and Motherland, more venerable than the heaven'.)

He opined that their movement was not a middle class movement and that they had contacts with Rash Behari Bose and Sun Yat Sen.[90]

90 Jadugopal Mukhopadhya, P-558-560

APPENDIX-III

A LIST OF REVOLUTIONARIES OF BENGAL CATEGORISED ON THE BASIS OF THEIR AGE, CASTE AND PROFESSION [91]

A categorization of the revolutionaries of Bengal on the basis of their age, caste and profession has been gleaned from the Sedition Committee Report. Those who have been convicted for waging war against the king, or those convicted for some special reasons, or those who were martyred in the period between 1907 to 1917, have been included in this list.

PROFESSION

Student	68
Teacher	16
Talukdar (Owner of a Taluk, landed estate)	19
Business	23
Doctor or compounder	7

91 Nalinikishore Guha, 2017. P. 190.

Clerk and government employee	20
Newspaper employee	5
Others	26

CASTE

Kayastha	80
Brahmin	65
Baidya (a class of physicians)	13
Mahishya (cattle rearers)	3
Koibortyo (mainly fishermen)	3
Baishya, Rajput, Tanti (weaver), Shudra	1 each
Others	7

AGE

10 to 15	2
16 to 20	48
21 to 25	76
26 to 30	29
31 to 35	10
36 to 45	9
Above 45	1

APPENDIX-IV

REVOLUTIONARIES WHO TURNED RECLUSE[92]

Many revolutionaries ultimately turned recluse. Here is a list of some of them:

Surya Kumar Sen	Nirbanananda (Ramkrishna Mission)
Radhika Adhikari	Swami Sundarananda
Shanti Mukherjee	Dinananda
Jatin Bandopadhyay	Niralamba Swami
Priyanath Dasgupta	Atmoprokashananda (Ramkrishna Mission)
Satish Dasgupta	Swami Satyananda
Nagendranath Sirkar	Sahajananda (Ramkrishna Mission)
Dinesh Das	Nikhilananda
Debabrata Basu	Progyananda

92 Nalinikishore Guha, 2017. P. 290-291

Naren Sen	Naren Maharaj (Ramkrishna Mission)

There are many others besides the above. And, of course, there is the stellar instance of Aurobindo Ghosh, one of the pioneers of the revolutionary movement, who later shifted to Pondicherry and gave up all political activities. He became renowned as Rishi Aurobindo who established the internationally famous spiritual centre, the Aurobindo Ashram. It is a striking feature of the movement that those who had offered themselves at the altar of revolution later turned into *sanyasis*.

BIBLIOGRAPHY

Bagchi Mani. *Bagha Jatin*, Published by Bhabesh Chandra Biswas, Kolkata, 1968.

Bhattacharya, Buddhadev (Ed). *Freedom Struggle and Anushilan Samiti*. Article by Niharranjan Ray. P. 24. Calcutta: Anushilan Samiti, 1979.

Damodaran, Vinita. "The East India Company, Famine and Ecological Conditions in Eighteenth-Century Bengal". In V. Damodaran; A. Winterbottom; A. Lester (eds.). *The East India Company and the Natural World*. UK: Palgrave Macmillan, 2014. Pp. 80–101, 89.

De, Amalendu. *Anushilan Samitir Ithihas* (1902-1947), Published by Anushilan Samiti Shotoborsho Udjapon Committee, 2002, Kolkata, Published in 2013.

Deuskar, Sakharam Ganesh. *Desher Katha*. Edited by Mahadebprasad Saha, Foreword by Ashok Chattopadhyay. Radical Impression, 2016.

Fieldhouse, David. "For Richer, for Poorer?", in Marshall, P. J. (ed.), The Cambridge Illustrated History of the British Empire. Cambridge: Cambridge University Press, 1996.

Guha, Nalinikishore. Banglay Biplabbad. Published by Radical Impression, Kolkata, 2017

Halder, Jibantara. *Anushilan Samitir Itihas*. Sutradhar Publishing. P. 29-30.

Kanungo, Hem Chandra. *Banglay Biplob Prochesta*. Published by Radical Impression, Kolkata, 2016

Lahiri, Tarapada. *Bharater Swadhinata Sangram O Nana Boiplobik Shorojontro Mokoddomar Itihas*.:Published by Radical Impression, Kolkata, 2022

Lahiri, Trapada. *Bharoter Swadhinata Sangram o Samprodayik Rajniti.* , Published by K.P.Bagchi & Co., Kolkata, 2nd Edition, 2005

Laushey, David M. *Bengal Terrorism and the Marxist Left.* In *Vivekananda Complete Works,* Mayavati Memorial Edition. Calcutta: Advaita Ashram, 1958. Chapter-1, P. 3.

Mukherjee, Prithwindra. *Bagha Jatin: Life and Times of Jatindranath Mukherjee.* New Delhi: National Book Trust, 2020.

Mukherjee, Uma. *Two Great Indian Revolutionaries.* Kolkata: Dey's Publishing, 2005. P. 171.

Mukhopadhyay, Jadugopal. *Biplobi Jiboner Smriti*. Published by Academic Publishers, Kolkata, 1982.

Roy, Suprakash. *Bharater Boipolobik Sangramer Itihas.* Published by Bharati Book Stall, 1949.

Sarkar, Sumit. *The Swadeshi Movement in Bengal 1903-1908.* New Delhi: People's Publishing House, 1994. P. 376.

Sen, Sailendra Nath. *An Advanced History of Modern India.* New Delhi: Macmillan, 2010. P. 235.

List of Acronyms

HRA	–	Hindustan Republican Army
HSRA	–	Hindustan Socialist Republican Army
IB	–	Intelligence Bureau
ICS	–	Indian Civil Service
IIL	–	Indian Independence League
INA	–	Indian National Army
SDO	–	Sub Divisional Officer